~101~
SCRIPTS
FOR STAGE, STREET, AND SANCTUARY

Compiled by Matt Tullos and Christy Marsh Haines

Church Street Press
Nashville, Tennessee

5201-09

~

Acknowledgements

All Scripture references are from the *King James Version* of the Bible unless indicated otherwise.

Scripture references marked NASB are from the *New American Standard Bible.* © The Lockman Foundation, 1960, 1962, 1963, 1968, 1971, 1973, 1975, 1977. Used by permission.

Scripture references marked NIV are from the Holy Bible, *New International Version*, copyright © 1973, 1978, 1984 by International Bible Society.

Verses marked TLB are taken from *The Living Bible*, Copyright © Tyndale House Publishers, Wheaton, Illinois, 1971. Used by permission.

101 Scripts for Stage, Street, and Sanctuary
Dewey Decimal Classification: 812
Subject Headings: Drama— Collections/Worship— Drama
Printed in the United States of America

ISBN 0-8054-9820-6

Pastor-Staff Leadership Department
The Sunday School Board of the Southern Baptist Convention
127 Ninth Avenue, North
Nashville, Tennessee 37234

Introduction

*A*s you thumb through this collection, don't be overwhelmed by the number of scripts. Don't try to do all of them in a month. Your audience will thank you for it. The ground rules for these scripts are simple. *Use them!* Photocopy them! Rehearse them! Perform them on stage! Perform them on the Street! Perform them in the Sanctuary! Just use them. We want the Good News found in this book to be heard. Hone your talent. Practice your gifts.

You may say, "There are many reasons why God shouldn't use me..." *You're right!* But don't worry. You're in good company. Moses stuttered. David's armor didn't fit. John Mark was rejected by Paul. Timothy had ulcers. Hosea's wife was a prostitute. Amos' only training was in the school of fig tree pruning. Jacob was a liar. David had an affair. Soloman was too rich. Jesus was too poor. Abraham was too old. David was too young. Peter was afraid of death. Lazarus *was* dead. John was self-righteous. Naomi was a widow. Paul was a murderer. So was Moses. Jonah ran from God. Miriam was a gossip. Gideon and Thomas both doubted. Jeremiah was depressed and suicidal. Elijah was burned out. John the Baptist was a loudmouth. Martha was a worry-wart. Mary was lazy. Samson had long hair. Noah got drunk. Did I mention that Moses had a short fuse? So did Peter, Paul—well—lots of folks did.

But God doesn't require a job interview. He doesn't hire and fire like most bosses because He's more our Dad than our Boss. He doesn't look at financial gain or loss. He's not prejudiced or partial. Not judging, grudging, sassy, or brassy, not deaf to our cry, not blind to our need. As much as we try, God's gifts are free. We could do wonderful things for wonderful people and still not be—wonderful. Satan says, "You're not worthy." Jesus says, "So what? I am." Satan looks back and sees our mistakes. God looks back and sees the cross. He doesn't calculate what you did in '88. It's not even on the record. Sure. There are lots of reasons why God can't use me or you. But if you are magically in love with Him; if you hunger for Him more than your next breath, He'll use you in spite of who you are, where you've been, or what you look like. I pray that as actors, artists, choreographers, and writers—we will step out of our limitations into the unlimitable nature of who God is. Then our passion for God and our passion to communicate Him will make mince-meat of our limitations.

Keep creating!

Matt

Dedication

This book is dedicated to a true pioneer in Christian Drama—Ev Robertson.
For the past 20 years he has paved the way for
dramatic excellence in the church.
May God continue to bless his ongoing ministry!

Table of Contents

Evangelism

Discipleship and Family

REACHING THE PEAK
by Matt Tullos

CELEBRATING SEX IN YOUR MARRIAGE
by Matt and Darlene Tullos

Worship

Ministry

Fellowship

ONE ACT

Scripts for Evangelism

THE BOOK
by Christy Doyle

God's sovereignty or human error...

Cast: *Clerk, Diana, Holly*

Props: box with Bible inside, bench, packages

Setting: *A typical busy department store during the holiday season. A woman is trying to return a gift at the service desk.*

Diana: Hi. I'd like to return something, please.

Clerk: Big surprise. OK. What department is it from?

Diana: Oh, I don't know. Do you have a book department?

Clerk: You don't know? Is it a book or not?

Diana: Well, yes it's a book. But it's a religious book.

Clerk: A book's a book. Do you have the receipt?

Diana: No, it was a gift.

Clerk: A gift during Christmas. Another surprise. OK. Let's take a look. *(She opens the box.)* A Bible? Real useful gift, huh? No wonder you're returning this. Sorry, I can't take it.

Diana: What do you mean you can't take it?

Clerk: It's not from our store. I don't blame you for trying to get rid of it, but it's not ours.

Diana: But it was delivered in a Paradise truck and it has your logo on the box.

Clerk: Look, lady. We are Paradise Department Stores. This is from The Paradise Store. Minor fact, but a big difference.

Diana: Are you sure? I don't think this gift was for me. I just want the right person to get it.

Clerk: Hey, it's not from our store. If I were you I'd think of some religious person you know, and I'd wrap it up and give it to them as a gift . . . save yourself a few bucks.

Diana: But it doesn't belong to me.

Clerk: Hey, it's a Bible. It's not like it's worth anything.

Diana: But it looks like it's real leather. It must have been fairly expensive.

Clerk: *(laughs)* A leather coat is expensive. A leather Bible is a joke. Did you ever think that someone might have sent it to you as a joke? Was there a card with it?

Diana: No, there wasn't.

Clerk: There you go. It was probably a gag gift.

Diana: Yeah, I guess you're right.

Clerk: Well, we've got a sale on slightly damaged angel ornaments in our holiday department. Why make this a wasted trip, you know?

Diana: Well—thanks anyway.

Clerk: OK. Don't forget to check out those angels.

Diana leaves, sits on a bench outside. Holly enters.

Holly: Diana! I can't believe I ran into you! I've been trying to get hold of you.

Diana: Holly! Hi. Boy, it's good to see a friendly face!

Holly: Oh, I know. The crazy holiday mob! I love to shop, but not when the amateurs are out. Hey, you didn't by any chance get a Bible delivered to you, did you?

Diana: Yes —is it from you?

Holly: Yeah, but it's not for you. I'm sorry. You must think I'm a kook—like I'd give my best friend a Bible for Christmas. Great gift, huh?

Diana: Well . . . who's it for?

Holly: It's for my brother, John. I sent you a gift from the same store. It's a great little book store. Anyway, John got your gift.

Diana: You're sending John a Bible?

Holly: Yeah. You're not going to believe this. John became one of those "born again Christians."

Diana: John?? The party person? John, the "I can hold more beer than a bottle" person?

Holly: Yeah. He says Jesus changed his life. Funny thing is, he *is* a much better person. He's really great to be around. Now, of course, when he starts to talk about "Jesus did this and Jesus did that," well, I think "stop, stop, stop!" But I'm so glad he found something.

Diana: How did he find that something?

Holly: Well, you know John. He's like you. He loves to read. So, he got a Bible out of the library, of all places. I guess he found God in a book.

Diana: I've never read the Bible, have you?

Holly: No. I like novels, something with a little romance. The Bible is like Shakespeare. I never did like classical stuff. But, the lady in the book store suggested a modern language Bible. She said it's easy to read. So, tell me the truth. What did you think when you got that Bible?

Diana: Well, I knew it was a mistake. But, it sort of freaked me out.

Holly: Yeah. Why is it that religious stuff sort of makes you feel itchy?

Diana: It's not that. It's just that it arrived on the anniversary of my mother's death. And I never told you this, but my mom worked for a Bible publishing company.

Holly: Ooh . . . that's spooky, all right.

Diana: In the hospital before she died I said, "Mom, what can I do for you?" She said, "Honey, read the Book."

Holly: What book?

Diana: I don't know. She just stopped breathing after she said that.

Holly: That's weird. Maybe God's trying to tell you something, huh? Well, I've got a ton of shopping to do.

Diana: Yeah. *(shows the Bible to Holly)* Here's John's gift. Holly, would you mind if I brought it over to John? I haven't seen him in ages. I'd love to talk to him.

Holly: Sure. Thanks. It would save me the trip. I'll bring your real gift over tonight.

Diana: Great. I love you. *(They hug good-bye. **Holly** exits. **Diana** hugs the book and pauses before she speaks.)* OK, Mom. I'm listening. I never did listen very well when you were here. I miss you, Mom. I want to see you again one day. To tell you the truth, I'm scared I won't. You used to say this was a history book with lots of mystery. Mom, I want to find out. You always did pick the perfect gift. Merry Christmas. *(She smiles.)* God, if You're somehow letting her hear all this, tell her I love her.

***

ALL SOULS COME CLEAN
by Matt Tullos

A celebration of God's everlasting love for everyone!

Cast: Actor #1 (female), Actor #2 (male)

Actor #1: For God so

Actor #2: Greatly

Actor #1: Loved the world, that He gave His only

Actor #2: Unique

Actor #1: Begotten Son, that whosoever believes in

Actor #2: Trusts in

Actor #1: Clings to

Actor #2: Relies on

Actors #1 and #2: Him——

Actor #1: Shall not perish, but have eternal

Actor #2: Everlasting

Actors #1 and #2: Life...for God so greatly loved.

Person who is not speaking turns back to audience.

Actor #1: My name is Susan Jones, and I'm sixteen years old. To be honest, my life is just one big mess. About three months ago, I found that I'm pregnant. I was hoping my parents would be supportive. It took a lot of guts to not have an abortion. Instead, they have put me away as a disgrace. My friends have deserted me. I feel as if even God has deserted me. I wonder if there even is a God. No one cares about me...no one.

Actor #2: My name is Willie Cook, and I'm sixteen. Two years ago my parents were granted a divorce. It certainly wasn't granted by me. Dad used to come home from work when I was just a kid, and we'd toss the ball around for hours. It was so special, that time that we spent together. I saw him a few weeks ago for the first time in about a year. He reached out his hand to me and said, "How's it goin', Son?" I just stared at him. He looked surprised that I didn't just throw my arms around him and say, "It's goin' just great, Dad." Finally, I said to him, "Who do you think you are? You aren't my father. You gave up. I hate you." Why did I say that? I don't hate my father. I love him.

Actor #1: My name is Barbara Courtney, and I'm seventy-eight years old. My husband died two years ago, just three months after our 50th wedding anniversary celebration. We had a wonderful marriage. Oh, I was far from being the perfect wife, but he loved me, faults and all. We had three beautiful children. Tommy, the oldest, lives in Los Angeles with his family. He has such a nice family, and a good job. Our daughter, Angela, is a missionary in Argentina with her husband, Jerry. And our youngest son, Don, was killed in Vietnam while serving his count...(*She breaks down.*) Oh, Lord, I do love You. It's just so lonely here in Dallas. It seems as though most of my friends are with you. The children are so far away. I'm unable to go to Your house these days. I'm so weak—I feel as if even the church has forgotten me. I want to come home.

Actor #2: My name is Corey Wilkes, and I'm thirty-five years old. I found out four months ago that I have a terminal blood disease. I'm not expected to live more than eighteen months. Oh, please, don't feel sorry for me. I thank God for using this tragedy to wake me up. You see, I'm a hardheaded guy. And yet, through this disease, Jesus has made Himself so real to me. I know now how precious my life has really been. Life as a servant of God is ten times more fulfilling than a life of running away from Him. I know that this disease is far from being terminal in God's eyes. Everlasting life means . . . forever.

Actor #1: For God so

Actor #2: Greatly

Actor #1: Loved the world, that He gave His only

Actor #2: Unique

Actor #1: Begotten Son, that whosoever believes in

Actor #2: Trusts in

Actor #1: Clings to

Actor #2: Relies on

Actor #1 and #2: Him

Actor #1: Shall not perish but have eternal

Actor #2: Everlasting

Actor #1 and #2: Life . . . for God so greatly loved.

Actor #2: Wife abuser

Actor #1: Child molester

Actor #2: Midnight cruiser

Actor #1: Stock investor

Actor #2: Honored marine

Actor #1: Associate dean

Actor #2: Chain Smoker

Actor #1: Flunky

Actor #2: Hash toker

Actor #1: Junkie

Actor #2: Redneck man in Ku Klux Klan

Actor #1: Congressional page

Actor #2: Victim of Aids

Actor #1: All souls come clean

Actors #1 and #2: John 3:16.

HAVE YOU HEARD ABOUT ZACK?
by Nancy Sheffey

The following is a contemporary look at what lifestyle evangelism means and how powerfully it persuades

Cast:
Samuel B. Solomon, a well-dressed, Wall Street-type about 35 years old
Jason R. Feinstein, a loud, bragging, ego-centric, money-loving, deal-making (you get the picture) guy, older than Sam
Extras (including a waiter)
Voice-over Narrator

Props: *tables, chairs, minimal table settings, glasses, drinks, waiter tray, restaurant tab, pocket address book, expensive looking watch*

Setting: *A small, intimate, expensive restaurant/bar at late afternoon. The set could be arranged with a few small tables, and some extras sitting there pantomiming. Soft restaurant music plays in the background throughout. The light is on Samuel B. Solomon, who sits center stage sipping a drink and obviously waiting for a friend as a narrator reads Luke 19:1-10, the passage telling the story of Zacchaeus, from a contemporary version of the Bible.*

As soon as the Narrator (live or taped) finishes the Scripture passages, Jason R. Feinstein enters from the audience, stopping to shake hands with the audience as if he knows them, talking loud and boisterously as he goes (i.e., "Yo, Jake! How are ya! Good to see ya!...Mrs. Cathcart, you are looking great, doll! Enjoyed the party last week! Didn't come to for days!" etc., etc.) Finally shakes the hand of an Extra at a table near Sam's and says...

Jason: Frank! How are ya?

Extra: *(correcting him that his name is Stan)* Uh...that's Stan.

Jason: Oh, yeah! Stan, right! Close though, huh? *(Then as he gets to Sam at the table, Jason says in stage whisper)* Hard to remember the ones ya can't stand. *(loudly again)* So, Sammy, how goes it? You're looking sharp. *(Handling Sam's lapel, he flips his head in a gesture reminiscent of their boyhood.)* How's Hedy? The kids?

Sam: Good, good, Jason. Yours? *(Throughout this first small talk part, Jason continues waving and nodding to patrons; some acknowledge him, some don't.)*

Jason: Fine, great. You've seen my oldest, Ben, in the paper? *(Sam doesn't seem to know.)* That Venson trial last week. *(Waiter comes forward and Jason signals to Sam's drink as Sam remembers.)* The kid made some lawyer. Can't handle his money, though. Leaves that to the old man! *(pridefully whacking himself in the chest)*

Sam: You're the best, Jason.

Jason: And you catch on quick! *(leaning forward, speaking in stage whisper.)* Speaking of which, did you get that tip I sent over?

Sam: Got it, Jase. *(Waiter brings drink.)*

Jason: Well? Well? How many shares did ya get?

Sam: *(uncomfortably mumbles)* Two hundred.

Jason: *(loudly again)* Only two hundred? C'mon, Sam. Small change, kid. You gettin' soft?

Sam: No...no...it's...

Jason: *(interrupting)* Don't trust my information?

Sam: No, Jase...just being...careful.

Jason: Careful is middle income, Sam. What do I always tell ya? You gotta get bigger. Think bigger! Buy bigger!

Sam: Yeah, yeah, I know. So, did you hear about Zach?

Jason: *(This brings Jason out of his jovial mood.)* Zach? What's he up to now? I haven't heard a word from him since that Smithers deal. The bum. You know I got him that job with Lynch.

Sam: Yeah? *(not surprised)*

Jason: That's right. I know some people. Got him right in. We gotta stick together, you know. If the altar boys from the East side can do it, so can the boys from Temple Beth El *(begins singing a Hebrew song rather loudly and Sam is embarrassed saying, "O.K., O.K. 'Enough, Jase." Some patrons frown and Jason laughs, enjoying himself immensely.)* O.K.! O.K.! Whoa! The patrons are feisty! So what's up with Zach?

Sam: He's gone clean.

Jason: *(For the first time since he's been on stage, Jason is completely still. He slowly leans forward and says incredulously)* What? That little weasel? Clean?

Sam: I'm serious, Jase. He met this guy, a famous teacher and lecturer...

Jason: *(teasing)* You been sniffing some bad stuff, Sammy boy?

Sam: No, really! This guy...

Jason: *(interrupting)* What guy?

Sam: His name is Jesus Christ.

Jason: *(Quickly pulls out his "book" and turns to "C" and begins scanning for the name, mumbling "Christ" over and over.)* Naw, I don't have Him...who is He? Some Hubbard protege?

Sam: I don't know, really. His father was in construction in a little place...uh...Nazareth.

Jason: Nazareth? Yeah, well, little dumps like that have produced some great ones.

Sam: Yeah. Wasn't Boesky from a fishing village in Europe?

Jason: *(insulted)* Hey! Yours truly's from Boynton Beach! They don't get much smaller. So, what happened...IF I'm gonna believe this.

Sam: Well, Zach's been hearing about this Jesus Christ and keeping up with Him. So he hears He's coming to the city. Going right down Park Avenue and all these people are around this guy.

Jason: For what?

Sam: He...they say He...does and says incredible things, Jase.

Jason: Yeah? *(voice heavy with sarcasm)* Like what?

Sam: Like miraculous, unexplained things.

Jason: Hey! Can He make a million on the Exchange in a minute? Huh? *That*, my friend, *(planting his finger in Sam's chest)* is a miracle!

Sam: Yeah. Anyway, there's always a lot of people around Him - some bodyguards, I guess, and so Zach wants to see Him. So he gets in his limo and pulls around and parks it on 27th Street by the Toreador.

Jason: His limo? *(sneering with disgust)* You know he only has that thing 'cause he's small enough to get lost in a Fiat. Waste of money, that car...

Sam: Yeah. So, he's parked there watching, and down the street comes this Christ, and He gets to the corner of 27th and stops. He turns and looks right at the limo and says, "Zach,"...like He knew him, like He'd met him before...and he says, "Zach, come out of there because I'm going to be staying at your place while I'm in the city." Can you believe that? I mean, this guy is famous. He could have stayed anywhere in the city with anybody in the city! And He goes to that thieving low-life's place!

Jason: You're believin' this, Sam!?!

Sam: Zach swears...*(stops abruptly)*...that is, if Zach swore, he'd swear it.

Jason: He didn't know this Jesus Christ?

Sam: No! He'd never seen Him before. So Zach gets out of the car and starts walking with Him to his penthouse.

Jason: Walking?!? Zach lives on 89th, doesn't he?

Sam: Yeah. Zach said he kept hailing cabs, but the cabbies wouldn't stop. Just flew by like they didn't see him! And all the way they're walking, this Jesus is talking to him like He's known him all his life! He knew Zach's family, his childhood, all about his business deals—*(He pauses.)* He knew *everything (pointedly)* Zach had ever done.

Jason: Everything?

Sam: All of it.

Jason: *(trying to take all this in—then in a low, conspiratorial voice)* He knows somebody. This Jesus Christ is big. Very big. He wanted a payoff, right?

Sam: No, nothing like that. Zach said He never talked about money.

Jason: *(frustrated)* So what did He want? His wife? His house? *(With each sentence he is getting louder.)* His job? His soul? *What*?!

Sam: He just wanted to stay at Zach's place.

Jason: *(long pause)* You believe this?

Sam: I wouldn't, Jason. I wouldn't believe a word from that worm...except for one thing. *(leans forward)* You remember that Opti-brand's merger six years ago? Zach took me for twenty thousand on that.

Jason: What? You never told me that! That miserable...

Sam: *(interrupting)* Wait, wait. He gave me the twenty thousand back Tuesday. *(Jason reacts to this, but Sam goes on.)* and an extra eighty thou because he said he'd cheated me out of it. Said he was making good, paying back everything.

Jason: Cash?

Sam: Cash.

Jason stops dead, looks at Sam, then jumps up to leave, but Sam grabs his arm.

Sam: Where you going?

Jason: To call Zach. The weasel owes me eight grand!

Sam: You don't have to call him, Jason. You'll get the money. *(Jason sits back down.)* If you lost it to him dirty, he'll give you four times the amount.

Jason: Of course it was dirty. I taught him everything he knows. *(calculating his "take")* Mmmmm — thirty-two thou—not a bad return.

Sam: He's been making good all over town, Jase. He's sold the limo, the yacht, the house in Tahoe. He's setting up charities all over the place and telling everybody he knows about this Jesus Christ.

Jason: You're joking? This is Zach we're talking about here?

Sam: I'm serious. It's real.

Jason: Naw...

Sam: He's taken away Ruth's credit cards…

Jason: *(freezes a moment)* It's real.

Sam: So, I'm going to meet this Jesus Christ.

Jason: *(brightens)* He's still here?

Sam: Not in the city. He's in Jersey.

Jason: Whoa! He's definitely not worried about His rep!

Sam: Wanna come?

Jason: What? Now?

Sam: He's big, Jason. There's got to be something to it. You know…you *knew* Zach. Something's happened to him and I'm going to find out what it is.

Jason: *(considering)* Wait a minute. Didn't you say this Jesus knew everything Zach had ever done?

Sam: Yeah. Yeah, He did. But the Christ guy told him He didn't care about that. Said it didn't matter.

Jason: *(pausing, trying to figure it out)* He's big, all right. Too big. Something don't fit…I don't like it. Who does He know that I don't know?

Sam: Somebody big.

Jason: Yeah…*(The suspense is too much for him.)* Look…uh *(checks his expensive watch)* I'll tell ya what, Sammy. I have a few hours here. I'm gonna do this thing with ya, Sam. *(stands, puts drink down)* We'll take your car. I gotta make a phone call. Meet ya in the parking lot…silver Jag, you know the car. *(Turns and makes his way out mumbling.)* He must have some seminar, this guy. Or some connections. Well I wanna know who *He* knows!

*As **Jason** gets up, a waiter has come over and **Sam**, realizing he's been stuck with the tab again, smiles and shrugs at waiter, pays, and follows **Jason** out.*

JUST A MOMENT
by Gail Blanton

A portrait of time passing

Cast: *Leader, Mr. Patrick, Nurse, Younger Woman, Older Woman, John (man), Tom (man), Passenger, Agent, Mother, Two Children, Judge Preacher, Teacher, Ryan, Witness, Convert, Small Son, Dad, Husband Wife, Nanny, Mrs. Todd-Baker, Bill (teen), Betsy (teen), Person as arms of the clock*

Props: *Doll in blanket, four chairs, airline ticket*

Setting: *Actors position themselves at the time indicated in a large circle representing a clock. Use levels so the clock will be slanted toward the audience enabling everyone to be seen. One **Person** stands center, his outstretched arms forming the hands of the clock. At the conclusion of each time sequence he should move, robot-like, rising slightly on his toes and jerking to the next time space. If performed as part of a worship service, he may stand behind the podium. There is no need to disturb the pulpit furniture. **Leader** may stand to either side or at a level above and behind the clock. Each group freezes when not speaking.*

Leader: "Behold I tell you a mystery; we shall not all sleep, but we shall all be changed, in a moment, in the twinkling of an eye, at the last trumpet: for the trumpet will sound and the dead will be raised incorruptible, and we shall be changed." *(1 Cor. 15:51-52, NASB)* We shall be changed. Forever. In a moment. At the last trumpet, yes—a mystery. Yet we are no strangers to change. In the tick-tock, chock-full, moments of the clock, our lives are forever changed, in a moment.

*12:00: (**Mr. Patrick**—directly in front of him stands a **Nurse**, so that he is hidden from audience. She lifts a baby (doll) wrapped in a blanket toward the audience.)* Jason Lee Patrick, born at exactly 12:00 noon. *(Nurse turns to **Mr. Patrick** and hands him the baby.)* Congratulations, Mr. Patrick. From this moment on, you're a father. *(He shows his awkwardness by reaching for the baby in several different positions before he finally gets a clumsy hold on him.)*

*1:00: (A **Younger Woman** hugs an **Older Woman** as she says)* What a moment! Congratulations, Mom! You're now a grandmother! *(**Older Woman**'s face is toward audience. While still in the embrace, she reaches up with one hand, extends a shaft of hair and rolls her eyes upward as if checking to see if it is gray.)*

2:00: **John:** I appreciate you doing my physical, Tom. It's a hassle having to do it every year, but the insurance company insists. Well, I've got to run. See you at the club Saturday.

Tom: Uh, just a minute, John. I don't know how to say this except straight out. I don't really like what I saw today. I'm afraid it could be a malignancy.

3:00: **Passenger:** *(waving airline ticket)* You don't understand, Miss. I've got to be on that plane!

Agent: I'm sorry, sir. If you had been here a moment earlier. . .

Passenger: But I have to—what's that they're saying? Terrorists on board Flight 396 on the runway . . .*(with a sense of tragedy as the impact hits him)* Oh noooo. Do you realize I could have been on board that plane?

*4:00: (Four chairs placed as car. **Mother** in front*

mimes driving. **Two Children** *in back argue.)*

Mother: Be quiet, kids. *(They continue arguing.)* Hold it down, I said! *(They continue.* **Mother** *turns head toward the back seat.)* Stop that this instant! *(As she turns toward front, she gasps and shields her face with her arms. All react as if they receive a jolt when the car is hit; then they slump.)*

5:00 (Two men, standing back-to-back. One is **Judge**; *one is* **Preacher**, *who faces the audience first. There is not an actual couple standing there.)*

Preacher: I now pronounce you husband and wife. What God hath joined together, let no man put asunder. *(Preacher turns his back to the audience,* **Judge** *faces the audience.)*

Judge: *(bangs fist on hand as if using a gavel)* Divorce granted. Alimony denied. Joint custody of the children until further order of this court.

6:00 **Teacher:** Nonsense, Ryan. Don't waste another moment thinking you're dumb and have no talent. Who told you that?

Ryan: *(No response; stands dejectedly with head down.)*

Teacher: Well whoever it was did not know what they were talking about. Now, let me show you the good things about this report and show you what you really do well.

Ryan: *(Straightens and grins.)*

7:00 **Witness:** Did you pray just now to receive Jesus into your heart as your Saviour?

Convert: Yes, I did.

Witness: Then according to this verse, what do you have from this moment on?

Convert: Eternal life.

8:00: **Small Son:** Dad, c'mere. Look at this.

Dad: Just a minute, son. I'm busy.

Small Son: Dad! Hurry up!

Dad: Just a minute. *(pause)* Now, what is it?

Son: Never mind. It's gone now.

9:00 **Husband:** Believe me, I didn't mean for it to happen. She was just so young and pretty and— available. But I love you and I love the kids. Can you ever forgive me? I. . .

Wife: One moment, please. What are you saying? *(dazed)*

10:00 **Nanny:** Hello, Ms. Todd-Baker. Have to work late again?

Ms. Todd-Baker: No, I didn't have to, but I really want that promotion, so I volunteered.

Nanny: I wish you had been here just a moment earlier. The baby just took her first step.

11:00 **Bill:** *(trying to pull* **Betsy** *close to him)* Just a minute. I'm not going to have to put up with this all evening, am I? I understood from the gang that you were cool.

Betsy: Well...

Bill: Come on, kid. Everybody else is doing it. Grow up.

Betsy: Well...okay.

Leader: Change in a moment; a moment of change. Passing and arriving, arriving and passing. The moments pass, or rather we must pass through the moments: wisely or wastefully, through good times or bad, growing or regressing, sinning or refraining. In choosing one thing, we refuse another, for each moment. So alike, and yet, by the impact of change and choice, each moment is different. Cherish its significance; savor its uniqueness. So reachable, then so irretrievable. Moment—the word itself means "important." In one moment it will be midnight. Do you know where your moments have gone?

Pause. Hands of the clock move to 12:00.

...AND THAT'S FINAL
by Jeff Atwood

Cast: *Two men A and B.*

A: You know, there's final exams, and "that's the final straw," and when you die, that's final.

B: Not necessarily, but there's the final out in a baseball game.

A: And my mom used to say "That's final," and when you die, that is final.

B: Doesn't have to be. Oh, and there's the last cookie in the cookie jar.

A: That's right. Someone always gets the last word in an argument, and death is the final part of life.

B: Uh, not for me. But there is always, "It's time for *Final Jeopardy*," and Jefferson's Furniture Outlet closing their doors for the final time.

A: Right, and death is final, and that's final.

B: No, it's not, but let me see, it's my turn now...

A: What do you mean? When you die, you die. Dead. Stone cold. Hard as a rock. Worm food, uh, R.I.P., "Hasta la vista Baby."

B: Doesn't have to be.

A: What are you talking about?

B: Just that death doesn't have to be final.

A: Like Shirley McLaine or something? What in the world are you talking about? Do you think we come back as another being from the planet Xantar? (*sings* Twilight Zone *show theme*) Doo-Dee-Doo-Doo...

B: Nope, it's really pretty simple.

A: What??

B: It's like this. Have you ever been to a funeral, or driven by a car accident?

A: Yeah, sure.

B: And what did you think of?

A: I guess I thought about dying...

B: And...

A: And I guess I was scared.

B: Right. See Death is just a bully. He's a scrawny little runt pretending he's the Terminator, when all he is is a runt puffed up with a bunch of hot air. 'Cause 2000 years ago Jesus Christ said I'm your friend, your big brother, and I'll take up for you in this fight against this puffed up runt called Death. 'Cause when you fight a bully, like Death, you need a big brother.

A: What do you mean?

B: I mean that Jesus came to this earth, became a man like you and me—well maybe a little different—went to the cross, looked Death square in the eye, played ball with Death on his own home court, and walked away the winner. Jesus beat up this bully called Death. Just like your question. Does death have the last word? Well, my big brother, Jesus said, "Not on your life."

A: So, death doesn't have to be final?

B: No, Man, death doesn't have to be final. Now the final out in the World Series, that's final. And the final play of the game...?

KAREN'S STORY
by Matt Tullos

Great for student evangelism

Cast: *Dad, Karen, Mom, Debi, Danny, Mary, Cindy, Teacher, Jesus*

*This short dramatic interpretation is a composite sketch of what many students are facing in their homes and schools. It takes on the style of readers theater by using focal points and by having the freedom to move swiftly from one time frame to another. However it is recommended that actors not use a script. All actors except **Karen** begin with their backs facing the audience. Each turns around as his character speaks and interacts with **Karen**.*

Dad: Karen, this is difficult to say. I'm sure you already know that your mother and I have really been going through some tough times. I've decided that it would be best for me to move out for a little while. I promise to visit every now and then. I guess what I'm trying to say. . . Believe me I don't want to lie to you. You know I'd never want to do that. But I doubt your mom and I — that we'll ever resolve things. She wants a divorce and — I do too.

Karen: Dad—I thought you'd be around. My birthday was last week. You didn't even call. I don't know if this letter will even get to you. Don't you—care for me? I'm your daughter. What did I ever do to—Why? I just want to know why.

Mary: Where did you get those jeans? They're practically antique. Is your mom still shopping at K-Mart? I don't see how you do it. I know that your mom and dad split up but get real! If you can't afford new stuff, maybe you should think about getting a job after school. It's getting embarrassing to be seen around you.

Mom: What's wrong with you! Can't you get a grip! I know why you spend half your life in your room with the doors closed. You try to hide it but I know. You hate me. Why don't you admit it.

Karen: I don't hate you!

Mom: Don't lie to me, Karen. You blame me for everything. Why don't you grow up and take some of the blame yourself. I'm not the only reason your dad left.

Danny: I just don't understand why. There's no reason for you to be afraid. I'm not going to hurt you. I'm frustrated. I need you. Why don't you just give in. I love you. What's wrong with it. If you truly love a person you should have the freedom to express it.

Karen: I was just hoping that —

Danny: Hoping for what? Hoping that I would just stick around and wait for you to make up your mind about whether you love me or not?

Karen: It's not a matter of love—

Danny: You don't even know what love is about! The only thing you care about is yourself. What about me? What about my needs?

Debi: I think you ought to know this. We've heard a lot of stories about you and Danny. Can't you see? He's using you.

Karen: He loves me and we're committed to each other.

Debi: I just hope you're protected because you aren't the first one, and if you want my opinion, you won't be the last.

Danny: I feel like we're a married couple. I need some space.

Dad: Karen, I really wish I could but there's no way. Money is really tight right now and the only possible way that you could make it to Seattle is by air.

Karen: I could drive.

Dad: Are you kidding? Look Karen, I've got to go. I'm leaving for L.A. Call me next week. No, that won't work. I'll still be on the road. You hang in there. I love you. Bye.

Karen: Sure Dad.

Danny: Somehow I knew it would come to this.

Karen: You lied to me.

Danny: We grew apart.

Karen: Why couldn't you at least let me know about Lisa. Everyone knew.

Debi: I hate to break this to you but—

Karen: But me.

Danny: Don't you get it, Karen? You're living in a dream world. The thing you're searching for doesn't exist. You can't expect people to live up to your fantasies of the perfect—

Karen: How dare you! How dare you talk to me about fantasies. You taught me to believe in them. You liar!

Danny: Nobody's perfect.

Karen: Will you please leave?

Cindy: Come on, Danny. We haven't got all day. (as they turn away from Karen) What a creep. . .

Teacher: You dropped out of the Drama Club. You flunked the written exam. And now you want out of the play? What's gotten into you?

Karen: I'm just tired of it. I don't enjoy it.

Teacher: I don't think you understand what you're asking me to do.

Karen: Please just sign the transfer slip.

Teacher: You really had me fooled. I thought you had real potential. Just remember . . . You back out here and you'll be a failure the rest of your life.

All the actors turn around and form a semi-circle around Karen.

Mom: You're to blame for this whole mess.

All: Why were you ever born?

Teacher: Go ahead. Do whatever you want to do. I really don't care.

All: You're a failure.

Dad: I'd love to, Honey, but this month is a real killer. Maybe after summer's over.

All: You're not worth my time.

Cindy: We don't know you very well, but we know enough to realize how totally mixed up you really are.

Mary: I hope you'll grow up one of these days but until then—

All: Please leave us alone.

Danny: I hate that it had to come to this but I've changed since we first met. I don't love you anymore.

All: (*Karen covers her head, moving back, trying not to be hit by all these words hurled at her.*)
Unlovable...Insignificant...Worthless...
Unlovable...Insignificant...Worthless...
Unlovable...Insignificant...Worthless...

*All freeze except for **Karen**, who continues to shield herself. **Jesus** enters.*

Jesus: Karen?

Karen: Leave me alone!

Jesus: Come here. Come to me.

Karen: You can't help me. Just let me die. I'm tired of my life.

Jesus: I will give you rest. I love you.

Karen: That's impossible. If you say you love me then you must not know me.

Jesus: Karen, please believe me. I know you. I know your every thought. Every moment I know where you are. I made every delicate cell and organ of your body.

Karen: If you know me that well. How can you even look at me. I'm so full of hate, greed, anger, failure, impurity. So full of sin—that's what they call it at church. They call it sin. That's me. That's who I am.

Jesus: Stop evaluating yourself by what the world thinks of you. I love you. I died for you. If you come to me, you will be a new person.

Karen: I can't live up to that! I can't be new.

Jesus: You're right, Karen. You can't. Not alone—there is no one who is righteous on this earth. Not even one! But come to me.

Karen: Why are you accepting me?

Jesus: It's not for you to understand.

Karen: I'm such a fool. I was so deceived and rebellious. I don't think I can live up to your—

Jesus: You don't have to live up. Just live. I saved you not on the basis of deeds which you have done to be righteous. I saved you by my love. Karen, surrender is much different than earning. I'm not asking you to earn it. I just want you to come to me. Come home, my weary child. Come home.

CHRISTMAS IS...
by Tim Shamburger
Simple yet powerful reading

Cast: *Six Actors or Readers*

One: Christmas is . . .

Two: Shopping and getting gifts

Three: Crowds and stockings and trees and those smells in the air

Four: Like the chestnuts roasting over an open fire and Jack Frost nipping at your nose

Five: Tinsel and ornaments and parties

Six: And that big bunny! *(Everyone looks at Six.)*

Two: I think that's Easter—Christmas has the big guy in the red suit.

Six: Oh.

One: And Christmas is . . .

Three: Watching the wonder in the eyes of a child

Four: As he sees "It's a Wonderful Life" for the very first time!

Five: Or seeing the gleam in the little one's eye

Two: As he sees the computer game he just has to have!

Six: And then as he watches the fireworks as we celebrate the birth of our nation and we sing *(starts to sing)* "Oh, say can you see, by the dawn's early light . . ."

Three: Whoa! That would be Independence Day.

One: And Christmas also is . . .

Four: Trying to decide who to offend this year by not sending them a card.

Five: Deciding which in-laws to go visit.

Three: Eating too much.

Six: Of that turkey and dressing and pumpkin pie as we thank God for the bounty that He provided, remembering the pilgrims and how they sat down with the Indians . . .

Two: Hold your horses, *you're* talking about Thanksgiving, whereas, *we're* talking about Christmas.

Six: Christmas?

Three: Christmas.

Six: Christmas?

Four: Yes, Christmas.

Six: You mean the day we celebrate that God came down to earth in the form of man so that He could live a perfect life and atone for our sins by His death on the cross? That Christmas?

One: Yeah, that's the one.

Six: Oh, I just didn't recognize it by your descriptions.

THE CHRISTMAS CARD
by Christy Doyle

A Christmas greeting from the past

Cast: *Larry and Ginny (young married couple)*

Props: *Two chairs, card table, Christmas cards, pen, newspaper, radio or boom box, box of Christmas cards, two stuck together, one with a note from Ginny's father*

Setting: *It is the week before Christmas. Ginny sits at a card table writing Christmas cards. Larry is reading the newspaper in a chair. Christmas carols are coming from a radio or boom box.*

Ginny: *(She starts to sing along with a song—off-key.)* I love this year's Christmas cards. I think they're the best ever. It's a good thing I shop for our Christmas cards early. I can't believe it's almost Christmas. I just love Christmas. Do you know why I love Christmas, Larry?

Larry: *(not interested)* Why, honey?

Ginny: Because it's the one time of year you can go into debt and it's okay. Shop, shop, and never never stop. Right, honey?

Larry: *(not listening)* Yeah, stop, stop, never shop. Sure, honey.

Ginny: Larry, you're not listening are you?

Larry: Sure I am, honey. You said you're going shopping. Have a good time.

Ginny: I can't go shopping now. I have to finish these Christmas cards. I have about a dozen left and then I'm finally done.

Larry: Okay, honey, have fun. Don't spend too much money.

Ginny: You have absolutely no Christmas spirit.

Larry: *(hearing this time)* Yes I do, Ginny.

Ginny: No, you don't or you would tell me to spend as much money as I want.

Larry: Now why would I want to do that?

Ginny: Because that's what Christmas is about.

Larry: Correct me if I'm wrong, but I thought Christmas was about "doing" for other people.

Ginny: That's what I'm doing—shopping for all those people.

Larry: This is truly a profound statement coming from the daughter of a minister.

Ginny: Why do you always bring my father up?

Larry: Because you're so different than he was.

Ginny: Why do I think that's an insult? Look, my dad became a minister when I was all grown up and look where it got him . . . dead and buried in the ground.

Larry: Your father died in a plane crash. He didn't have any control over that.

Ginny: Yes he did. He wouldn't be dead if he hadn't been going overseas to preach. Why was preaching so important anyway? I don't want to talk about this. I've got to finish these cards. Look, I'm almost done. *(She starts to count.)* . . . five, six, seven . . . oh, no!!

Larry: What's the matter?

Ginny: I've only got seven cards and thirteen names.

Larry: Well, just cut out some of the names.

Ginny: I can't. These are all people we have to send cards to. I know we've got a box of some old unused cards in the closet. Can you get it for me?

Larry: Okay. *(He exits).*

Ginny: Okay—well, maybe I can cut somebody out. Let's see —what about Gladys? We send her a gift anyway. Why does she need a card? Yeah, I can cut Gladys out—no, I can't. What about Marie? No, Marie gets insulted so easily. She'd kill us if we didn't send her a card. Oh, how about Danny and Linda? They didn't send us a card last year—but they did send us a poinsettia—no, I can't leave them out.

Larry: *(entering with a box)* Is this it?

Ginny: Yeah, great. *(She looks through the box.)* Oh, look! There's a whole box of Christmas cards. . . . Oh, no! I can't use these!

Larry: Why not?

Ginny: They've got Jesus on the card. I can't send a Christmas card with a picture of Jesus on it.

Larry: Yeah, you're right. Somebody might actually think you know what the holiday is all about.

Ginny: You can be sarcastic all you want, but I'm talking about business associates. Religion and business don't mix.

Larry: Why bother to send "Christmas" cards then?

Ginny: Oh, you're impossible! *(looking through the box)* Ick! Susie must have dropped glue at the bottom of this box. Everything is sticky and stuck together. *(She separates two envelopes that are glued together.)* Hey, look at this. It's a Christmas card that was never opened.

Larry: Who's it from?

Ginny: It can't be!!

Larry: What can't be?

Ginny: It's from . . . my dad.

Larry: What do you mean it's from your dad?

Ginny: The postmark is two years ago . . . the week before . . . well, before he died.

Larry: Open it.

Ginny: I can't. It's too spooky.

Larry: It's not spooky. It just got stuck in the bottom of that old box. Do you want me to open it?

Ginny: Yeah.

Larry: *(opens it and reads.)* "Dear Ginny. I know we can't spend this Christmas together. I'll be gone for quite sometime. But I want you to know that I love you more than you'll ever know. And Someone Else does too. I hope in the midst of all your shopping and Christmas cards you'll see the real meaning of the season. Jesus loves you and so do I. He's the reason that preaching is so important to me. I look forward to the day I get to see your pretty face again . . . Love, Dad."

The actors freeze.

_____

TRAVELIN' LIGHT
by Nancy Sheffey

Cast: *Two men, Traveler and Russ*

Props: Large backpack filled with various size rocks

Traveler enters. He is obviously struggling under the weight of a large backpack. As he approaches the front he encounters Russ. Traveler begins to falter and Russ runs to help him.

Russ: Here! You're going to fall. Let me help you with that.

Traveler: (*waving him off*) Naw, I'm fine. Don't need no help. (*He sits.*) I've been carrying this thing for so long that it's a part of me.

Russ: Really? How long's that?

Traveler: Since November 12, 1947.

Russ: Whoa! You've got quite a memory!

Traveler: I can do that. (*proudly*) I have quite a memory.

Russ: So what are you carrying in that thing anyway? (*Traveler looks at Russ suspiciously.*) Uh... sorry...the name's Russ. (*Russ holds out hand which Traveler ignores.*) Just curious about what you're packin'.

Traveler: Yeah... well...let's see here. (*He takes out a small rock. He takes it out deliberately with great pride and care.*) February 15, 1951. My father whipped me so hard that my back bled. He was a mean old cuss, my old man. Whipped me every time he got a chance. He thought he could beat me into submission like an old mule, I guess.

(*takes out another treasured rock*) June 3, 1967. My boy comes to me and says that he's quitting college. Says he never wanted to go into engineering. Says he did it for me. For me! Can you believe that? I gave him the chance I never had. I worked hard for years at the garage and he quits! He went to tech school to learn auto mechanics.

Russ: What's that one?

Traveler: Aww...my wife was in on it. She said that he always did want to work with his hands like. . .

Russ: Like his Dad?

Traveler glares at Russ then continues, looking for a certain rock. He pulls out a small pebble.

Traveler: Man hit my old dog, Sadie, last year. She got loose and ran down the road. I was standin' right there and I saw it all. All that fellow could say was, "I'm sorry." I loved that old hound.

Russ: Kind of small isn't it?

Traveler: Yeah, but I like to carry it around with me anyway. I've got smaller ones than that! (*He pulls out a large one.*) Jack. (*bitter tone*) Good ole Jack. Thought he was my partner. My friend—we were in business together for eleven years.

Russ: What happened?

Traveler: I found out that he was trying to bring in another partner without my knowin'. Another friend of ours—they both denied it. Especially Jack. He swears to this day that—

Russ: You still see him?

Traveler: Who? Jack? Yeah, I see him. He's been trying to patch it up with me for years, but I won't have any of it. No sir! I trusted him...once. I won't be fool enough to do it again.

Russ: Just can't forgive him though.

Traveler: Oh, I forgive him. I know what the Bible says about that. And I do forgive him. I even told him so.

Russ: But you can't forget.

Traveler: Not going to. (*He smiles with pride.*) Got a gift for rememberin'.

Russ: So the pack's full of this...

Traveler: Rememberin's. That's what I call 'em.

Russ: But these...uh...rememberin's, as you call them...they're useless. And they sure make for a heavy pack. Must force you to slow down and stop to rest all the time.

Traveler: (*as he packs*) I don't mind stoppin'. It gives me time to think.

Russ: And remember.

Traveler: Right.

Russ: So why are you carrying it around?

Traveler: Why?

Russ: Yeah. It's not worth anything. All it does is weigh you down.

Traveler: (*thinks about it as if he'd never thought about it before.*) 'Cause...because it's mine. It gives me comfort somehow.

Russ: Looks like you'd be better off without it. You could make better time. Get a lot more done.

Traveler: Feelin' good about myself is more important than all those things, fella.

Russ: Feeling good about yourself?

Traveler: Sure! When I stop and rest, I unload my pack and—

Russ: All of it?

Traveler: Sometimes, but most of the time I just take out a few things. Rememberin' makes me feel good. A man needs to remember. If you had a pack, you'd see.

Russ: (*thoughtfully*) You know sir, I used to have one.

Traveler: You did?

Russ: Yeah, but I got tired of the weight. I realized that it wasn't doing me or anyone else any good. I saw that I didn't need it anymore and I could do a lot more without it. It was great to finally have it off my back. I was free to move on. (*Pause. **Russ** stands to leave.*) Well, speaking of moving on, I'd better get going. Nice seeing you. (***Traveler** is contemplating.*) Well, God go with you brother.

Russ turns to leave.

Traveler: Hey! Your pack. (***Russ** turns back to him.*) You say you left it?

Russ: Yeah. Left it with a Friend. He collects them. He offered to take it so I left it with Him.

Traveler: Just like that?

Russ: Just like that. I could introduce you to Him.

Traveler: Is it far?

Russ: No. Not at all. Come on.

Traveler: Well, I guess it couldn't hurt.

Russ: You're right about that.

Traveler shoulders pack and they leave together.

THE COVER-UP
by Ralph Dewey

Feeling guilty? A bag won't help, but Jesus will!

Cast: *Lucinda and Everett (any age), or could be played with two males or two females, or two puppets*

Props: paper bag large enough to go over head

Lucinda: *(She pops up with a bag over her head.)* I'm so embarrassed! I would like to dig a hole and crawl in it. That's why I'm wearing this bag, so nobody will know who I am.

Everett: Who are you? I mean, WHAT are you?

Lucinda: Go away, Everett; I don't want anyone to see me!

Everett: Your voice sounds familiar but you don't look like anyone I know. Are you a bank robber?

Lucinda: Of course I'm not a bank robber!

Everett: Do you have a skin condition and that's why you are wearing that bag?

Lucinda: No, I don't have a skin condition. If you must know, I'm embarrassed that I've never told anyone about Jesus. So I'm hiding from God.

Everett: That's silly. You can't hide from God. He knows everything. Take that bag off.

Lucinda: I guess you are right. *(Everett looks away while Lucinda takes off the bag.)*

Everett: *(Everett looks and is shocked.)* Egads!!!!

Lucinda: Why are you screaming? It's me, Lucinda!

Everett: Oh, it's you. For a minute there I thought you had bags under your eyes.

Lucinda: Don't be silly, Everett. Help me with my problem.

Everett: Instead of wearing a bag over your head, talk to God about your problem. Let Jesus take control of your life. Remember that we learned that in church? Let's go and look it up in the Bible. *(Everett exits.)*

Lucinda: Why didn't I think of that? *(She exits.)*

DEAD FAITH
by Randall and Arinée Glass, and J. Scott Reynolds

Faith is action

Cast: *Two actors, #1 and #2, or two puppets*

#1: Yeah, I'm really glad that we decided to go this way.

#2: Me too.

#1: Well, we can't just stay here, we need to go on. And I guess that means taking this bridge.

#2: This bridge? *(looks over edge)* Long way down, if this bridge breaks.

#1: It won't break.

#2: Yeah, maybe, but it sure looks old.

#1: Of course it is, but He wouldn't have sent us this way if it wasn't the right way. Let's go. *(starts across)*

#2: *(looks fearfully)* You go ahead. This is a major cliff.

#1: *(from the other side)* Come on, I made it! It's great.

#2: No, I think I'll just stay here.

#1: What's the matter don't you trust the bridge?

#2: Sure I do, I saw you go over.

#1: Then what's wrong? Come on over.

#2: No, I would rather stay here.

#1: If you stay there, you'll die. There's no food or water there. Come on, if you believe it will hold you, come on over. I did.

#2: Are you judging me? I *believe*! I have faith. Why do I have to *show you*?

#1: Well, anyone can *say* they believe. But can *your* belief get you safely over this cliff?

A SPECIAL DAY
by Christy Doyle

A super Superbowl Sunday sketch!

Cast: *Married couple, Char and Jack*

Setting: *The kitchen/living room area of a typical home on Sunday morning. Char is making coffee.*

Props: *Use minimal, pantomime most. Table, two chairs, newspaper, soda can, bag of sour cream chips, bag of regular chips*

Char: Well, Lord, today is the day. Today is the day that Jack promised to go to church with me. I know he's going to love it. To tell you the truth, I never thought he'd agree to go with me, but he did. He said, "Char, as soon as football season is over, I'll go with you." Well, I know all those play-offs are over. I guess they just played off all those games. *(excited)* Today is going to be such a special day!

Jack: *(Entering from outside. He's been out to get the morning paper. He speaks with an unseen neighbor offstage before entering.)* Hey, Bob! We're gonna kill 'em, huh? They'll probably end up calling it Super Choke Sunday, huh? . . . What? . . . Of course I'm going to watch it . . . I haven't missed a *(insert name)* game all year . . . What did you think —I was going to church or something? . . . Yeah . . . See you later.*(Jack enters kitchen and Char hands him a canned soda.)*

Char: Hi, Sweetie.

Jack: Hi, Honey.

Char: So, today's a pretty special day, huh?

Jack: It sure is . . . and you know what? It makes me proud you're aware of it too.

Char: Thank you, Jack. I'm proud of you, too. And you know what? I'm excited for you, too.

Jack: Why, Char, that's really sweet.

Char: So, what are you going to wear?

Jack: Well, I thought I'd wear this. *(He's in sweat clothes.)*

Char: Oh . . . okay.

Jack: What's wrong with this? I like to be comfortable. *(He grabs a bag of potato chips.)*

Char: You're right. You should be completely comfortable. Clothes shouldn't matter one bit.

Jack: Of course they shouldn't. It's not like anybody is going to be staring at me.

Char: Oh, of course not!

Jack: *(He bites a potato chip.)* Oh . . . sour cream. Why would anybody put sour cream in a potato chip? Anything with the name "sour" should not be allowed in food. Do we have any regular chips?

Char: No, but we've got some chocolate covered pretzels.

Jack: Chocolate covered pretzels?? That's ladies' luncheon food.

Char: Jack, they make chocolate covered pretzels for men and women.

Jack: Not this man.

Char: Hey, who were you talking to before?

Jack: Bob.

Char: So, did you tell Bob what a special day today is?

Jack: I didn't have to. He already knew.

Char: Really?

Jack: We've been talking about it for weeks. *(Jack searches for food.)*

Char: Oh, Jack! I'm so proud of you. You're even telling your friends.

Jack: Hey! This must be my lucky day. I found some regular potato chips.

Jack begins stuffing the snacks into his pockets.

Char: Jack, I know you're a novice at this, but aren't potato chips rather loud?

Jack: Loud? Yeah . . . I guess, but the crunching will be drowned out by all the screaming.

Char: Screaming? Oh, Jack, this isn't that kind of church.

Jack: Church? What are you talking about?

Char: Jack! You promised to go to church with me today.

Jack: Whoa—not today! It's Superbowl Sunday.

Char: But the playoffs are over.

Jack: Right. And the winners are in *this* game. It's the biggest game of the year. There's football on all day. I'm sorry, Char, but it's a very special day and the pregame shows should be starting right about now.

Char: Oh well, that's OK. You know what I'm going to do?

Jack: What, Hon?

Char: I'm going to watch the game with you.

Jack: You are? Ah . . . don't you have some shopping to do? Maybe you need to go to church; you could pray for me or something.

Char: No. This is my gift to you.

Jack: Honey, this is not a good day to watch football.

Char: It's the perfect day. I'm going to do this for you. I love you.

Jack goes to the couch and uses the remote to turn the TV on. There is no actual TV. The actors direct their gaze at an imaginary TV between them and the audience.

Jack: Why is there a picture but no sound? Every channel is like this! After we just spent all that money for this big screen TV! Oh, this is great! Probably the best game of the year and I can't hear it! Maybe I can go to Bob's.

Char: *(on the couch with him)* You mean you don't want to spend time with me? *(She looks coyly at him?)*

Jack: But, Char —all right—at least I can still watch it. Those guys talk too much anyway. But look, Char, I think it's great you want to get interested in football, but you can't ask dumb questions, okay?

Char: Okay. I won't ask dumb questions. So, which team is ours?

Jack: We don't have a team. You pick a team you like and that's your team.

Char: Okay. Ummm . . . let's see . . . we have the (insert color) team or the (insert color) team. I like (insert color) but (insert color) was one of my school colors . . .

Jack: Wait a minute! You don't pick a team because of the colors of their uniforms. This is not a coloring contest. You're for the (insert team's name).

Char: Is that the team you're for?

Jack: Yes, it is.

Char: Oh, good. Then we can be happy and sad together.

Jack: Oh, look at this! They have a pregame interview with (insert name of prominent player) and I can't even hear it.

Char: Oh, I love that suit! I wish you'd wear a suit like that.

Jack: There's an idea! Why don't you go to the mall right now and buy me a suit just like that. . . and take your time.

Char: No, Jack. This is a special Sunday and we're going to be together.

Jack: Great. Oh, man! Here are some clips from past games and I can't hear it!

Char: Why is that guy running backward?

Jack: To cover the receiver.

Char: Oh. Which one is the transmitter?

Jack: This is going to be a long afternoon. (pause)

Char: So, how did football get started? (He looks at her.) It's not a dumb question—it's an historical question.

Jack: No, it's the wrong question. (He watches TV intently.) Oh man, that guy's always getting sacked.

Char: Getting sacked? You mean he . . .

Jack: Don't even ask.

Char: So why do they call those guys (insert name)? (Jack looks at her annoyed. He hands her a bag of potato chips and tells her to eat. She starts singing a popular TV commercial of the day which has obviously come on the screen. He glares at her.) I like that commercial.

Jack: I did until now. Eat. (Char begins to eat the chips loudly, biting down on them in an exaggerated way.) Do you mind? I'm trying to listen.

Char: But there's no sound.

Jack: I know there's no sound. I'm trying to concentrate.

Char: (She watches intently) Oh! I can't believe that guy jumped on top of that man. How do you watch this game. It's so violent!

Jack gets up and starts to leave.

Char: What are you doing?

Jack: I'm doing something before I get violent.

Char: What do you mean?

Jack: I'm going to get dressed. We're going to church.

He exits.

Char: Thank You, Lord. I knew when I got up this morning it was going to be a special Sunday. I can see the power of prayer really works. I've been praying for years that Jack would come to church with me. Oh, thank You, Lord, for the TV sound thing. That was a nice touch. If You can turn off the sound on the TV, You can change his heart.

Scripts for Discipleship and Family

Clouds and Fire Who Needs 'em!

by Gail Blanton

Be careful about what you ask for!

Actor is SR. As he makes nervous mannerisms, he looks at a door SL and then looks away; repeats several times before he speaks.

Well, as I was telling You yesterday, Lord, I have to make a decision today and I was really hoping to get some guidance from You. There's that door right there, see it? I really don't know if I should walk through it or not, Lord. Would You please just show me? I've been trying to decide, and I may be a little dense or something, but I hardly ever hear You say anything. I don't know why it has to be so hard to find out what You want me to do. Boy, in some ways those Old Testament people had it made. A pillar of cloud guided the Israelites during the day and a pillar of fire at night showed them right where to go. Why not me, Lord? But, I don't guess You do that sort of thing today. Well, Your will be done.

He starts toward the door, but begins to squint and sway. Stops.

Hey! What's going on? What's all this fog all of a sudden? I can't see a thing. (*Tries to fan imaginary cloud away.*) Come on, I'm in a hurry. (*Stands on tiptoe and tries to look over; lies on floor and tries to look under; rises and extends arms straight out in front, feeling as he resumes walking.*) Now where's that door? It's gotta be here somewhere. Beep-beep, coming through! (*Fans again.*) Oh, will you get out of here! (*Instantly he can see again.*) Oh, great, it's gone. Now we'll get somewhere.

Starts to walk toward door again. Suddenly jumps back as if he stepped on hot coals.

Ow! What was that? (*Examines floor in front of him, shrugs, starts again; jumps back even more gingerly; stamps feet.*) Ouch! What in the blazes— (*examines soles of shoes; puts palms up as if to a wall and jerks them away; spits on one hand and plunges it in, jerks it out and slings it in pain.*) Blast it! What a time for a heat wave. Right in front of my door, too. Always a hassle. Why me, Lord? But they say you can't stop a good man, especially one in a hurry. Sooooo, grin and dare it!

Covers his head with his jacket, dashes through imaginary fire, screaming; immediately drops to floor and rolls over and over. Stops right in front of the door; lies on floor and looks up at door.

Well, what do you know about that? I guess this means . . . yeah, I'll go through it. (*hand on doorknob or jamb*) What a great feeling; what assurance! Amen. (*Said in a singing manner, in the tone of "toodly-doo," as he goes through door.*)

GOOD HEALTHY PEOPLE
by Darrell C. Cook

A comical parable of health

Cast: *Mrs. Johnson, Nurse/Narrator, Paul, Aaron*

Props: *Five chairs, small table, clipboard, three hymnals*

Setting: *Mrs. Johnson is seated at one end of a row of four chairs placed at center stage. Nurse is sitting at a small desk and holding a clipboard, stage right. Aaron and Paul enter stage left, slightly bent over and holding their stomachs.*

Aaron: This must be it.

Nurse: May I help you?

Paul: Yes, we wanted to know if this is the doctor's office.

Nurse: Yes, would you like to sign in?

Aaron: No, of course not!! We're not sick! Come on, Paul, let's sit down.

Aaron and Paul sit next to Mrs. Johnson. She coughs. Aaron elbows Paul so they can move farther away from her.

Paul: But Aaron, I thought we were sick.

Aaron: We're not sick!

Paul: But if we're not sick, how come we're holding our stomachs?

Aaron: I said we're not sick!

Paul: But Aaron, if we're not sick how come we're sitting in the doctor's office?

Aaron: We're not sick! We're sitting here in this doctor's office so everyone will know how well we are.

Paul: Oh!? *(puzzled look)*

Nurse: Mrs. Johnson, the doctor will see you now.

Mrs. Johnson exits stage right. Aaron smiles and nods. Paul follows her with his eyes and longs to go in and see the doctor.

Paul: There went Mrs. Johnson. Now tell me again why we can't go see the doctor.

Aaron: If we go see the doctor, everyone will think we're weak. Everyone will think we have problems. If we just sit here, everyone will think we're good healthy people who don't need a doctor.

Nurse: *(Steps forward to become Narrator.)* And so each day for the rest of that week, Aaron and Paul went to the doctor and just sat in his office so everyone would know how healthy they were. Except for Sunday, since the doctor's office was closed, they decided to go to church.

Mrs. Johnson, Aaron, and Paul are seated listening attentively. After a few seconds, they simultaneously reach for their hymnals and stand. They pantomime singing the hymn of invitation.

Paul: I think I need to go forward and see the preacher.

Aaron: You don't need to do that.

Paul: But Aaron, I know my heart's not right with God.

Aaron: You don't need to do that.

Paul: Hey Aaron, there went Mrs. Johnson. Now tell me again why I can't go see the preacher?

Aaron: If we go up to see the preacher, everyone will think we're weak. Everyone will think we have problems. If we just sit here, everyone will think we're good healthy people who don't need . . . who don't need . . . God? Who am I trying to kid? I *do* need God.

Nurse: *(Steps forward again to become Narrator.)* Jesus said, "It is not the healthy who need a doctor, but the sick. I have not come to call the righteous, but sinners to repentance." *(Luke 5:31, NIV)*

HE ASKED US TO GIVE
by Matt Tullos

A dramatic challenge to give

Cast: *Girl, Teenager #1, Teenager #2, Teenager #3, Woman #1, Woman #2, Man #1, Man #2, Man #3*

Girl: He asked me to give. I don't have very much money but Jesus gave everything for me.

Man #1: He asked me to give and it wasn't easy. The drought this past summer had destroyed a third of my crops, but Jesus has never left us alone without hope for tomorrow. Without food and provision.

Woman #1: He asked me to give. And I'll gladly do so. My life was a total wreck before I felt the love and compassion of the church. I'll give with joy because Jesus is the one who brought me the joy. He pulled me out of a pit of despair. Hallelujah!

Teenager #1: My first part time job! And believe you me! I had plans for that money. But as I thought about my parents, about the sacrifice that they've made for years and years. I knew that it was right to give. He asked me to give.

Man #2: I had never seen a man like him before he came to our village. He didn't know our language very well but his smile showed us his heart. He told me where the joy came from. He told me about a man named Jesus. Now I know. For the first time in my life I understand! "Why did he come, how could he afford to be here?" I asked. He simply said, because someone gave.

Teenager #2: I wanted to go to this camp with my friends. But my parents could really care less. But someone gave and so I went. For the first time in my life I understood what Jesus did for me. I accepted Christ. I have everlasting life.

Woman #2: I was at the end of my rope. My four month old baby was starving to death. I had no hope, but as the sun rose the next morning, I saw a man who invited me to come to a newly opened clinic. There was food and medication. There was hope! I found Jesus through their sweet compassionate eyes. My child is alive because someone gave.

Teenager #3: I went on a summer missions assignment.

Man #3: We built a church.

All: And through giving, we worshiped our Savior and our Lord!

WHAT DO I DO NOW?
by Pamela Clampitt

A comical sketch about discipleship

Cast: *John, David, Automated Voice (live or pre-recorded)*

Props: *Telephone on small table, two chairs, Bible stuffed with religious literature, small wastebasket*

Setting: *John is sitting by the phone reading some religious literature that has been stuffed in his Bible; sighs; and begins talking earnestly to himself.*

John: Boy, I hope I can do all the stuff You want me to do Lord. This is all so new to me; it's all kinda scary. *(looking up)* I mean, I'm glad I made the decision to make You Lord of my life. I know it was the right thing to do, but what do I do now? *(Finds a sheet of paper; he stops and examines it. Reading out loud)* CHRISTIAN HELP LINE 1-800-HE-HELPS. Huh, sounds interesting.

He dials the number. A pre-recorded cheery telephone voice answers.

Automated Voice: Welcome to the Christian Help Line. To proceed, please press one on your touch tone telephone. If you are not calling on a touch tone phone, please hold for a Christian service representative. If you know your party's extension, dial now. Please don't hang up, as your call will be processed in the order it has been received.

He presses one.

The pre-recorded voice says:
 If your Christianity is not working properly press 2 now.
 For service organizations, press 3.
 To confirm an appointment, press 4.
 For general information, press 5.

To speak to a Christian service representative, press 6.
 To hear menu again, press 7.

John: *(puts hand on chin and thinks)* Hmmmm

Automated voice continues:
 If you need more time, press 8. *(pause)*
 If you need more time, press 8. *(pause)*
 If you need more time, press 8. *(pause)*

John: Well, I guess I should find out about service organizations. *(He presses 3.)*

Automated Voice:
 To select singles, dial extension 111.
 To find out about Missions on the Moon, press 1213.
 For Christian Calisthenics, press *(in an aerobics instructor's voice)* and 1-2-3-4.

John: *(disappointed as he hangs up phone)* I never knew this was gonna be so hard. All I wanted to do was talk to someone and find out what I should do.

David: *(walking quickly and sees John)* Hey John, *(shaking hands)* How's it going? You look kinda down, are you doing okay?

John: Well, I guess I'm okay. You know I'm really excited about coming to know the Lord. And I want to do all the right things. I saw this thing called the Christian Help Line. Here, do you want to see it? *(Shows David the flyer; David takes it and looks at it.)* When I called all I got was a recorded message. I just wanted to talk to someone and try to get some direction.

David: Looks to me like the direction you're looking for is right there in your hand. *(Points to John's Bible.)*

John: Really? *(opens the Bible)* I just thought there were a bunch of stories about Jesus in here. I've been trying to read a little, but . . .

David: There are real instructions and insights in here.

John: Really!!!?? Well, where should I start and what should I do?

David: *(showing John the book of John)* It's always good to start with the book of John and then read these books back here. *(pointing to Paul's letters)* There are some good commentaries in the library that might help you. *(pause)* You know, John, you're doing just fine in your Christian walk. All the direction you need is in this Book. Just take your time. Let the thoughts sink in and then you'll know what to do next, because God will lead you.

John: Wow, it's that easy?

David: It really is easy. The hard part is doing what He asks you to do. *(pause)* But He'll be there to help you through it all.

*They exit together. As they leave **John** wads up the flyer he read earlier and throws it in the trash.*

THIS LITTLE LIGHT
by Matt Tullos

Has Satan already blown out the light of your church?

Cast: *Reader #1* and *Reader #2*

Reader #1: We loved the light so we built a church around it to shelter it from the cold, dark world.

Reader #2: And every Monday night we take it out to visit those who saw the light last Sunday.

Reader #1: We have matchbooks that we carry with us, but we're afraid to use them for fear that something might catch fire and we wouldn't be able to control it.

Reader #2: So we leave the candle at the church where we can visit it whenever we want.

Reader #1: We love our light, but it seems these days that the light is getting dim...perhaps because it's running out of oxygen due to the walls we've built around it.

Reader #2: Every now and then I wonder what would happen if we opened the door and let the fire warm and the light shine, but we've grown quite accustomed to the darkness.

Reader #1: Hide it under a bushel? No.

Reader #2: We'd much prefer hiding it in a church...

Reader #1: We know that Satan would never find it there—would he?

Pause, next line to be sung.

Both: Don't let Satan... *(they pucker up their lips as if to "blow it out.")*

THE AUDITION?
by Kari L. Todd

Casting for the Christian

Cast:
Director's voice
Narrator
18: An actor going through the motions.
19: An actor going through different motions.
20: An actor trying any motions.
21: An actor who finds he doesn't need any motions.
22: An actor who finds that motions aren't the key.
Two Extras

Props: *Bible, tracts, detective hat, fake gun, environmental props, sign to carry*

Director's Voice: *(echo)* Numbers 18-22...Please report to stage one. Numbers 18-22...Please report to stage one. Final call. Warm-up time of three minutes. Prepare please.

All actors go through their warm-up procedure. Ad-lib to the ridiculous. Example: stretches, vocalization, silly noises, Shakespearian and/or ballet-type movements.

Narrator: *(Comes on stage; all actors freeze in the midst of warm-ups. To audience)* Anyone involved in theatre or music will understand the process of going through an audition. Finding just the right motion to get "in."

Some people and even some Christians think that you have to go through just the right motions for God...

(walking by the appropriate auditionee)...Saving the world in a mad frenzy without time for love...

Ridding the globe of every "evil" religion or differing belief...

Perhaps even going so far as to try and reach God through the metaphysical or some other abstract form...

Some people, even some of you, have bought into the idea that going through the motions is the way to Christ...But is it?

*(**Narrator** leaves stage and **all actors** resume.)*

18: *(to 20)* Are you ready for this?

20: *(in deep yoga concentration)* Ohmmm...

21: Like any of us can ever know what's expected...

18: I think I've got it this time, though.

19: Reliable sources?

18: I contacted the best.

19: What about the Instructions?

18: Never trust just the Instructions; there's always the chance... *(cut off by 22 who is rushing in late)*

19: You're right...I'll do it my way...

22: Am I too late?

18 and 21: *(uninterested)* No.

20: Ohmmm... Ohmmm...

18: I hope I make it.

Director's Voice: Number 18, call time. All others will follow in sequential order. *(to 18)* When you are ready...

18: *(Comes center stage as if the Director is seated in the auditorium.)* Hello? *(peering into the light)* I'm number 18 and I will be going through this piece accompanied by the Houston Symphony Orchestra. My rendition of the motions for Redeemin' Ranger. *(Takes a breath to prepare and bows head.)*

Music 1: theme from "The Lone Ranger"

18: *(Ad-libs a wild and crazy run around the room with tracts in one hand and a Bible in the other. Some points that should be included: the "saving" of several people in rapid succession; the "baptizing" of someone with great ardor; the throwing of tracts to audience; and IMPORTANT, ignoring someone who needs help to go to the masses.)*

Director's Voice: *(as 18 comes back up on stage, out of breath)* Time!

18: *(going over to the actors)* Try and follow that! *(proud of himself)* Yea! *(The actors don't say much but continue in their warm-up.)*

19: Well, here we go... *(to the Director)* Good Morning. Today I will go through a new writing of "Mavericks with a Mission." *(to the audience)* With your indulgence, this is a very timely piece and needs the utmost attention. *(to Director)* I've also asked several others to assist me. *(to the audience again)* Please remember not to try this at home, kids. *(gets props ready—probably fake gun and hat)*

Music 2: theme from "Mission Impossible" or "Hawaii 5-O"

19 ad-libs ridding the world of evil and false religions while doing a dive and roll, shoot-'em-up-type action.

Director's Voice: *(cutting music short)* Time!

19 *Comes back to the stage in a "Rocky-type" stance. Several of the other actors applaud him lightly.*

22: *(to 20)* Excuse me...I don't think I understand. I thought this was how we got in...

20: It is, honey.

22: But I don't know what I'm supposed to do. What are you going to do?

20: Well, you see, first I...*(realizing)* Hey, you'll have to get your own stuff, Hon. These are my motions.

22: But I really want to work for him...

Director's Voice: Next. Number 20.

20: Hi! Okay. I'm not sure if this is what you're wanting or not. But I've seen a lot of people do it. So I said to myself, I said, "Hey, self! Look at everybody doin' that cool stuff." That's what I said...

Director's Voice: Now, please...

20: Oh. Yeah, right... *(gets out all her environmental props)*

20: *(Vocally ad-lib something about saving the world; the environment; peace between men during beginning of Music 3)*

Music 3: theme from "Star Trek"

20 continues ad-lib. At some point during ad-lib, two **Extras** *can come in carrying a sign such as "Save the homeless baby flying squirrels," and Number 20 should stop in mid-movement.)*

20: *(to the sign carriers)* Hey guys! Wait for me! *(Actors snicker, look concerned, and so on.)*

22: Glad she didn't show me those motions. *(to number 21)* Hey, can you help me? What am I supposed to do? I didn't know we had to go through all of this. I thought that you just gave...

21: Leave it alone, babe. It's all a scam anyway. Just watch me. I'll show him a thing or two.

Director's Voice: Number 21…

21: *(coming center stage)* I'm right here! Now look. Let's get one thing straight. I want in…no, I *deserve* to be in. Look at my crummy luck so far! *(as if a secret)* You know about all of it anyway, don't you? Got the best background check around. I'm serious. I'm not going to get up here and go through a bunch of motions for you. You can either take it or leave it right like it is! *(Stands back, proud and defiant.)*

Two beats

Director's Voice: Next.

21: *(shocked, then angry)* Wait a minute! How dare you! Don't you know who I am? I don't deserve this! What did you want? *(1/2 beat)* Forget it. *(leaving)* Fine!

22: *(comes forward slowly)*

Director's Voice: And you?…

22: I'm not sure what I'm expected to do…

Director's Voice: You have the Instructions?

22: *(nods)*

Director's Voice: Then proceed.

22: *(takes a deep breath)* First I want to give you this…

Music 4: instrumental music bed

22: *(Motions giving her heart to Christ; then taking her Bible and opening it, giving her life and her all. Music fades down but not away.)*

22: *(in prayer position)* I'm sorry that's all I know.

Director's Voice: That's all you need. Come in—I'll teach you the rest line by line…

~

I Am Not Ashamed
by Pamela Clampitt

A dramatic interpretation to "I'll Tell the World that I'm A Christian"

Cast: *Apostle Paul, Two Soldiers*

Props: *Scroll, quill pen, stool, small table, bowl of food*

Paul: *(writing on a scroll and talking to himself)* I, Paul, "thank my God upon every remembrance of you. . . being confident of this very thing, that He which hath begun a good work in You will perform it until the day of Jesus Christ!" *(Phil 1: 3,6, KJV)*

Soldiers enter with a small bowl of food.

Paul: I pray that Your love may abound more and more.

Soldier 1: Here Paul, your rations for the day.

Paul: *(puts down pen and graciously takes food)* Thank you, Claudius!

Soldier 1: *(to other soldier)* What did I tell you, he is different.

Soldier 2: He's not like any others we've seen around here.

Soldier 1: *(mocking and mean)* Paul, I just don't understand you. You have such a good attitude. *(in a mocking voice)* Thank you, Claudius. You're not at all like the other prisoners.

Paul stands and explains gently to the soldiers.

Paul: It's what I was telling you before. I rejoice because Christ is in my life. He has changed me. I was placed in prison for preaching the gospel of Christ, but this place does not stop me from spreading the good news of my Savior. Whatever the circumstances, I am content to know and obey Christ. I am not ashamed of the gospel! I want to tell everyone about my Lord and Savior. I'll tell the world about Christ and His love.

Sing "I'll Tell the World That I'm A Christian" (The Baptist Hymnal, 1991, No.553)

A BOWL OF BEANS
by Randall and Arinée Glass, and J. Scott Reynolds

True Love Waits

Adapted from: *Genesis 25:27-34*

Purpose: *To show the great loss in giving up moral purity for a moment's pleasure.*

Cast: *Esau, Jacob, Guy, Girl*

Props: *Bible, chair for girl, two chairs for car*

Setting: *Girl seated stage left, Jacob and Esau stage right, two chairs for car center stage*

Girl: *(to audience)* Boy am I excited! I have a hot date with a guy tonight! He is so cute. But you know I have a few minutes before he should get here—I think I'll read my Bible. *(Reads from Genesis 25:27-34)* "He said to Jacob. . ."

On other side of stage Jacob pantomimes stirring his pot of beans.

Esau: Jacob I am *so* hungry can I please have some of those beans? *Please?*

Jacob: Nope.

Esau: Come on Jacob—I am so *hungry!* Give me some beans.

Jacob: Bowl of beans for your birthright.

Esau: Bowl of beans for my birthright! Come on! What good is a birthright to me if I die right now of starvation!

Jacob: Bowl of beans for your birthright.

Esau: Oh, all right, you can have my birthright, just give me the beans!

Jacob and **Esau** freeze and then exit.

Girl: "Then Jacob gave Esau . . . So Esau despised his birthright." Man, isn't that stupid! He gave up his birthright, this precious thing, he gave it up for a bowl of beans. A momentary thing. Stupid!

Knock, knock, knock,—Guy at the door.

Girl: Oh! He's here! *(opens door)* Hi!

Guy: Hi! You look great!

Girl: Thanks!

Guy: You ready to go?

Girl: Yeah! Bye Mom!

They go to center stage car. Guy opens car door for Girl—he's acting very much like a gentleman—his excitement for the evening shows. He mimes driving.

Girl: *(After Guy is in car)* Oh! it's your birthday today. Happy Birthday! Have you had a good birthday so far?

Guy: Oh Yeah! In fact this could be the best birthday ever!

Girl: Really?

Guy: Yeah! Have you had a good day?

Girl: Yes, it's been great. Where are we going tonight?

Guy: Tonight I have something very special planned. I'm taking you to my favorite spot to go to be alone. I haven't taken anyone there before.

Girl: Oh really? It sure is dark out here.

Guy: Yeah! I like it that way. We're almost there. *(mimes parking the car)*

Girl: We're in the middle of nowhere.

Guy: Listen . . . it's so nice and peaceful out here. Look through the sun roof; look at the stars.

Girl: Oh. Uh, they're beautiful.

Guy: You know we've been dating for a while now.

Girl: Two months.

Guy: Yes, and I really like you a lot.

Girl: I like you a lot, too.

Guy: And tonight I was thinking, maybe we should take our relationship one step further.

Girl: What do you mean?

Guy: Tonight—I think we should go all the way. *(Guy freezes).*

Girl watches stage left as Esau comes back and begs Jacob to return his birthright.

Jacob: No! You gave a bowl of beans for your birthright. *(Then Jacob turns to Girl)* Bowl of beans for your birthright? *(Jacob and Esau freeze.)*

Girl: *(pushes Guy away and screams)* "No way! You're not getting my birthright for a bowl of beans!

Guy: What? What are you talking about? A birthright for a bowl of beans?

Girl: Well, before you picked me up I was reading the Bible, the story of Jacob and Esau.

Guy: Yeah? We studied about them at church.

Girl: But the story I was reading told of Esau giving up his birthright to fill his stomach. A birthright was something that was very special, and Esau gave it up just to satisfy his desire at the moment. His birthright for a bowl of beans. That's what we would be doing.

Guy: But listen, you don't understand. In the locker room at basketball practice all the guys talk about are how many girls they've had and the things they do on weekends. They are always kidding me about being a virgin.

Girl: Listen, whenever you want to you can become like them in five minutes, but they can never be like you again. God has given our purity to us as a special gift. He wants us to save it for marriage.

Guy: I guess it would be pretty stupid giving up your birthright for a bowl of beans. Let's go somewhere else.

Girl: Good idea. *(They freeze.)*

Jacob: *(unfreezes and asks the audience)* Bowl of beans for your birthright?

_____

SHELLI AND MOM
by Darlene Tullos

Too busy for the important things

Cast: *Mom, 10-year-old Shelli, Narrator*

Perhaps the thing that our kids need the most is our undivided attention.

Shelli: Mom, guess what?

Mom: (*reading, uninterested*) What Shelli?

Shelli: I wrote a new poem today.

Mom: (*distracted*) That's nice, dear.

Shelli: I think it's my best one yet. Wanna hear it?

Mom: Not right now, dear. I've got a WMU meeting today, and I've got a lot to do to prepare.

Shelli: Can I help?

Mom: No, Shelli, just give me some time alone.

Shelli: Oh, okay. I was hoping we'd have some time to talk.

Mom: Well, Honey, I'd love to, but your father has invited some business associates over for a little dinner party tonight, and I'm going to be rushed all day to get things done.

Shelli: Maybe I could help you cook!

Mom: No, dear, I don't think so. Maybe you could go over to Beth's house tonight. You always enjoy going over there.

Shelli: Not anymore. Things get too wild for me over there.

Mom: Oh nonsense. Beth is a nice girl, and her parents are fine people.

Shelli: But that's just it. See, her parents aren't home much anymore. They go out of town all the time and . . . (*She realizes Mom is not listening.*)

Mom: I'm sorry, dear. What did you say?

Shelli: (*pause*) Never mind, Mom.

Mom: Well, listen Dear, I've got my meeting to go to and some errands to run, and then I'll be home to start dinner. And you're going to Beth's house. That will work out just perfect. Now don't forget your chores. I won't have time to vacuum and dust when I get home. See you later, Dear. I love you.

Shelli: (*disappointed*) Sure, Mom. Bye

*Mom turns back to audience. **Shelli** looks hurt. Both freeze.*

Narrator: "Little children, let us not love with word or with tongue, but in deed and truth" (*1 John 3:18, NASB*).

BURNING THE CANDLE
by Rick Shoemaker

A great sketch for a Christmas candlelight service!

Cast: *Mr. Martin (businessman in suit); Mike (teenage boy in slacks and nice shirt)*

Props: *desk, papers, telephone, report, fast food meal in bag, box with candles inside, matches*

Setting: *Mr. Martin sits at a desk—obviously weary, talking on the telephone..*

Mr. Martin: Look, I don't want excuses, I want action. Understand? I don't care if it is Christmas Eve. If that report isn't on my desk by 6:00 this evening—well, just get it here! Merry Christmas to you, too! *(Hangs up the phone. Dials another number.)* Hi, Hon. Look I won't be able to make it home in time for the Candlelight Service. I know Susie has a solo. I really want to be there, but the boss has been pretty unhappy with me lately. I really need to get this work done. I'll try to be home by 10:00. I love you. Give Susie a kiss for me. Bye. *(Hangs up phone)*

Enter messenger boy, Mike.

Mike: Mr. Martin, here's that report you wanted from Mr. Preston. And the supper from Burger Whiz. Anything else sir? It's almost 5 o'clock.

Mr. Martin: Mike, I know it's late, but I really need a big favor. I haven't had a chance to do any shopping for my wife and, well, if you could run down and get a couple of gifts—perfume, a sweater, or something. *(Takes out wallet.)*

Mike: Sir, I'd like to help. I really would, but my family and I have plans. I'm an usher for our Christmas Eve service, and my family and I always open our presents after church.

Mr. Martin: I'll make it worth your while. Here's fifty bucks. Spend thirty on my wife and keep twenty for yourself.

Mike: I really can't, Sir.

Mr. Martin: Okay. You drive a hard bargain. Keep the whole fifty and here's another. Not bad profit for an hour's work!

Mike: Mr. Martin, I've got to get home. My little sister Betsy is singing a solo and I don't want to be late.

Mr. Martin: Mike, I'm really desperate! Last year, I gave Katie a fifty dollar bill for Christmas and I really need to get her a regular gift this year. You've got to help me.

Mike: Sir, can I say something?

Mr. Martin: Sure, what is it.

Mike: I've known you for a long time. I can remember when you used to spend a lot of time with your family and at church, but now . . . what's the point, if you're so unhappy?

Mr. Martin: The point? Listen, Son, the point is if you're gonna make it in this world, you gotta make sacrifices. That's just the way it is.

Mike: You mean you have to sacrifice your family and your God to make it in this world?

Mr. Martin: Who do you think you are to talk to me like that, Boy?

Mike: I think I'm your friend, Mr. Martin.

Mr. Martin: I'm sorry Mike. Truth is, I've been under a lot of stress and . . . I guess I've been burning the candle at both ends.

Mike: I understand. May I give you a present?

Mr. Martin: A present?

Mike reaches into a box and gives him a candle.

Mr. Martin: A candle?

Mike: I picked these up for the Candlelight Service tonight. Since you've been burning your candle at both ends, thought you could use a new one.

Mr. Martin: *(Long pause as he looks at the candle.)* Thanks, Mike. (**Mike** leaves. **Mr. Martin** dials the phone.)

Mr. Martin: Hey, Bill. Sorry I lost my temper. Don't worry about that report. It will wait till after the holidays. Go on home and have a Merry Christmas. *(Hangs up. Dials again. Looks at his candle.)* Hi, Honey. I'll be there after all—I'm glad, too. Katie, I'll be home soon. *(Hangs up.)*

Gets up from behind desk and kneels in prayer.

Mr. Martin: Lord, It's been a long time since I let my light shine. From here on out, this candle is yours. *(Lights the candle.)*

Leads to lighting of all other candles.

SUNDAY NIGHT-LINE
by Tim Shamburger

Investigating a parable

Cast: *Todd Kepple, Joe Phool, D. Siple, Mr. Smith Voice (good for Puppets)*

Todd: Good evening, America, I am Todd Kepple and this is Sunday Night-Line. Tonight's story revolves around a recent tidal wave that hit the shores of Wahoo-Wahoo, Hawaii. We will be interviewing some of those who were affected by the wave and some of those who were surprisingly spared damage. First up, Joe Phool. Mr. Phool, would you assess the damage done to your home.

Phool: Todd, I have to tell you, it was somethin' awful. The entire second story is gone, and the walls around the first story seem to be missing as well. You see the winds came and they beat against the house, and the rains came, and well, the house fell.

Todd: Mr. Phool, if you will just hold on, we also have with us a Mr. Siple.

Siple: D. Siple.

Todd: Right. Mr. D. Siple, will you describe the storm from your perspective.

Siple: Certainly, Todd, you see the winds and the rains came just as Mr. Phool said, but my house, which is just next door, did not fall.

Todd: And what do you attribute this to, Mr. D. Siple?

Siple: I really don't know. I'm sure that Mr. Phool followed the guidelines for building just as I did.

Todd: What about it, Mr. Phool?

Mr. Phool: Of course. Whatever he did, I did. I just know it.

Todd: Gentlemen, we also have the building contractor who has done a survey for Mr. Phool's insurance company. Mr. Smith, what did you find?

Smith: Well Todd, it seems that the configuration of the edifice in question, that being the domicile of the first party, was in line with the specifications with only a slight variation from the edifice owned by the party of the second part.

Todd: Come again?

Smith: The houses were the same— with one exception.

Todd: What was that?

Smith: It seems that Mr. Siple–

Siple: D. Siple

Smith: Right. It seems that Mr. D. Siple built his house on a rock. And the rains descended and the floods came and the winds blew and beat upon the house; and it fell not: for it was founded upon a rock.

Todd: And Mr. Phool did not build his house upon a rock?

Mr. Smith: No, Todd, he did not. He built his house upon the sand. And the rains descended and the floods came, and the winds blew and beat against the house; and it fell and great was the fall of it.

Phool: Now wait a minute. Are you saying that my house fell because of a poor foundation?

Todd: I believe, Mr. Phool, that is exactly what he is saying. Mr. D. Siple, I would like to commend you on your wisdom in building on a solid foundation. And that is all the time we have tonight. Join us next week on Sunday Night-Line.

Voice: No one can lay any other foundation than that which is already laid, Jesus Christ.

THE MOST IMPORTANT BOOK
by Scott Icenhower

A puppet sketch for children introducing them to Bible study

Cast: *Puppets 1, 2, and 3*

Setting: *Library.* **Puppet 1 is reading, 2 enters.**

2: Hey, what are you doing here?! *(offstage response—"shhh!")* Sorry—*(softer)* what are you doing?

1: I'm reading about airplanes. Did you know that the first planes had four wings? They were called bi-planes.

2: Well that's interesting, but why are you reading about them?

1: Because I want to fly one someday, and I need to know all I can about planes. So I gotta read up on the subject.

Puppet 3 enters reading a book while walking, and runs into puppet 2.

2: Hey watch where you're walking! *(offstage response, "shhh!")* Sorry. *(softer)* What are you doing?

3: Hello, I'm sorry I ran into you like that, but I was reading this great book on doctors and I . . . .

2: Why?

3: Because I want to be a doctor someday! Oh, look, this chapter tells about your tonsils.

1 and 2 lean over to take a look at the book.

2: *Gross!* *(offstage response, "shhh!")* Sorry, *(softer)* You guys are serious about this stuff! So if I wanted to know more about Abraham Lincoln. I should read a book about him?

1 and 3: Of course!

2: And if I wanted to read more about telephones I should read a phone book! Get it? *(starts laughing)* or, if I wanted to learn more about matches I'd get a matchbook, or how about cookies?— a cookbook *(more laughter).* No, wait, how about worms? . . . . bookworm! *(offstage response, "shhh!")* Sorry! *(starts calming down)*

1: Boy you sure are funny. Look *(points to wall clock)* it's almost time for our Sunday School party. Do you want to come with us?

3: Yeah, come on. You'll have fun! What do you say?

2: Well, okay, but what do you do at a Sunday School party?

1: Well, there will be food.

3: And games. You'll meet a lot of people. And have a good time, plus a Bible study.

2: Bible study?

3: Yeah, as Christians we want to know more about God and what He has to say to us, so we read the . . . .

2: So if you want to know more about planes and medicine, you read a book about them; and if you want to know more about God you read . . . .

1, 2, and 3: The *Bible*!

1: Now you got it.

3: I'll say, come on. *(All start to exit.)*

2: This will be great! *(offstage response, "shhh!")* Sorry! *(All exit.)*

WHO'S CALLING?
by Marsha Pursley

I f God was on the "friends and family" plan

Cast: *Carol, Gail, Chris, Kari, Terri, Policeman, Voice*

Props: *Two small tables, two telephones, one lamp, fingernail polish, tissue, sound of phone ringing*

Setting: *Stage left Carol is sitting at a table with a phone on it, doing her nails. Stage right is a table with a phone and a lamp, for use individually by the rest of the cast. As they sit down, they turn on the lamp before dialing Carol's number. When they hang up the phone, they turn off the lamp.*

Voice: Often people ask, if God is *real*, why doesn't he contact us in a *real* way. . . in an audible way? If He's *real* why doesn't He just pick up the phone? But even if He did, would we listen? Would we speak? Or would we still be too busy, too careless, or too shameful to listen, to be still, and to seek Him?

Carol's phone rings.

Carol: Hello. . .Hello. . . Must be Jesus again. If this is Jesus, I would appreciate it if You'd call back later. I'm kind of tied up right now. Thanks. Bye. *(She hangs up.)*

A few seconds later. . .phone rings.

Carol: Hello.

Gail: Hey Carol. Are you going to the Shawn's party tonight?

Carol: *(excited)* I wouldn't miss it for anything.

Gail: What are you going to wear?

Carol: I haven't decided yet, but I want to look my best for Chris. He's picking me up later. We won't be staying for the whole party, if you know what I mean.

Gail: I understand perfectly. He's the best looking guy in school. Did you know Shawn has bought a keg of beer for this party? His parents are out of town.

Carol: *(surprised and uncertain)* No. . .I didn't. Who bought it? He's not old enough.

Gail: His cousin. Why, do you have a problem with that?

Carol: Well. . .I. . .

Gail: *(cutting her off)* Don't worry; nothing is going to happen.

Carol: *(more assured)* You're right. See you there.

Gail: Bye.

Carol: Bye.

The phone rings again

Carol: Hello. . .I'm sorry. I think I said that this wasn't the best time to call. Could you please call back, or better yet, I'll call you Sunday.

The phone rings.

Carol: Hello.

Chris: Hey, Babe! Are you ready for the party?

Carol: Can't wait. When will you pick me up?

Chris: I'm going over to Shawn's house first and have a few beers before I come by. Did you know he bought a keg?

Carol: Yeah. Gail told me. *(concerned)* Are you sure you should be doing this? Why don't you wait till I'm with you and I can drive?

Chris: *(a little angry)* What's with you? I don't need a designated driver. I won't drink that many anyway.

Carol: I'm sorry. You're right.

Chris: I'll pick you up at nine o'clock.

Carol: Okay.

Chris: Carol, don't forget to tell your parents you'll be home at 1:00, and we'll leave the party early and spend some time to ourselves.

Carol: *(excited)* I'll wear your favorite black sweater.

Chris: *(excited)* I can't wait. I love you.

Carol: I love you, too.

Chris: Bye.

Carol: Bye.

Carol gets up and twirls around the room as if she's deeply in love and excited.

The phone rings again.

Carol: Hello. . . I'm sorry I just don't have time right now! Good bye! *(She hangs up with a bang.)*

The phone rings.

Carol: *(angrily)* Hello!!!!!

Kari: *(uncertain)* Carol—uh—it's me, Kari.

Carol: *(feeling sorry)* Oh—hi, Kari.

Kari: I was just calling to see how you were doing. You haven't been to Sunday School in a while and I just wanted to check on you.

Carol: Well—I—wasn't feeling too good last Sunday so I stayed home, and the week before that I. . .

Kari: *(cutting her off)* You don't have to explain anything to me. I know it's hard to be there every week. I just got to thinking about camp last summer and all the things that happened in our youth group. There were a lot of decisions made for Christ.

Carol: Oh yeah—that seems so long ago. Camp was a lot of fun.

Kari: Camp was fun. We all learned how Christ is always there for us and "calling" on us to do the right thing. That's part of the reason I called you. There are several of us going out to the movies tonight. Do you want to come?

Carol: Well, I already have plans.

Kari: Are you going to Shawn's party?

Carol: *(hesitating)* Chris asked me to go.

Kari: *(disappointed)* I understand. Have a good time. Be careful.

Carol: *(feeling bad)* Thanks—bye.

Kari: Bye.

Carol: *(saying to herself and feeling guilty)* Why did she have to call? I know the difference between right and wrong.

The phone rings again

Carol: Hello. . .Why are you doing this, Jesus? *(She hangs up.)*

The phone rings again.

Carol: *Hello*!!!!

Terri: *(slightly crying)* Carol—I'm sorry to bother you but...

Carol: *(rude)* What's wrong now, Terri? Why are you crying?

Terri: It's my mom and dad. They're fighting again.

Carol: *(annoyed)* What about *this* time?

Terri: Same old thing—money, the house, Dad's job. . .

Carol: So why don't you leave for a while?

Terri: I don't have any money for gas for my car. Besides, where would I go?

Carol: *(hesitating)* Well, you could come over here but—I have plans.

Terri: I just wanted someone to talk to so I don't have to listen to them argue.

Carol: Terri, I'd love to talk but I have to do some—homework before I leave, so I'll see you later.

Terri: Sorry I called. . .

Carol: *(She hangs up the phone hard.)* Excuse me. I've got better things to do than listen to her problems. She needs to find someone else to talk to besides me.

The phone rings again.

Carol: Hello. . .this isn't funny anymore. What do you want? Don't call here anymore. Leave me alone. *(She slams down the phone.)*

The phone rings again

Carol: *Hello*!!!

Police: Is this Carol White's residence?

Carol: Yes. Who is this?

Police: This is the Metro Police Department. Are you Carol White?

Carol: Yes, I am.

Police: Are your parents home?

Carol: No, not right now. They went out to eat; they will be right back. What's wrong?

Police: Well, Miss—do you know a Chris Sanders?

Carol: Yes. Why?

Police: We found your phone number in his wallet and we need to get in touch with his parents. Do you know where they might be?

Carol: They're out of town. Is he all right?

Police: Do you know how to get in touch with them?

Carol: *(persistent) Is he all right???*

Police: Miss—he died in a car wreck tonight. He had been drinking. . .

(Carol hangs up, devastated and talks to God.)

Carol: *(looking up)* Why did You let this happen? Chris wasn't a bad person. . .He loved me. *(Pause. She falls to the floor on her knees.)* This can't be happening. . .my life is ruined. No one will ever love me the way he loved me. . .I trusted You. I made a commitment to You. Why are You punishing me? If You could only tell me. . .talk to me. . .help me. . .call me. Oh Lord. . .

The phone rings.

Blackout

Optional: The choir can sing "Jesus Is Tenderly Calling," (The Baptist Hymnal, 1991, No. 316).

ON THE LORD'S SIDE
by Matt Tullos

Character sketches of valiant believers

Cast: *Eight Actors (two men, two women, plus four of either), or could use with* **Puppets.**

Actor 1: *(as Daniel)* They said that I shouldn't pray to the only true God. I was a young man with a bright future in the palace of the king. Other subjects were jealous and sought to destroy me. I prayed. I broke the law, and the punishment was harsh; I was thrown into a deep hole filled with hungry lions. But those who wanted to kill me forgot one thing—I was on the Lord's side!

Actor 2: *(as Paul)* Beaten, scourged, and chained, my friend and I were thrown in jail. The people inside the cell thought we might bleed to death. In the eyes of the jailer and our fellow inmates, it was really no big deal. Two religious fanatics...that's what they thought. As we sang praises to God, it was as if our joy in Christ could overcome anything. From deep within the foundation of the earth we heard a rumbling. They left us to suffer and maybe even die, but they forgot one thing—we were on the Lord's side!

Actor 3: *(as Mary, mother of Jesus)* He searched for us day and night. He would have no rest until he found us. He lied to friends, slaughtered babies, and wouldn't give up until he saw the death of my child, God's Son, Jesus. He had many sleepless nights, many schemes, but he forgot one thing—we were on the Lord's side.

Actor 4: *(as a citizen of Israel)* The armies were astounded by the miracle, but they thought that Pharaoh was even greater. But they forgot one thing—we were on the Lord's side.

Actor 5: *(as Corrie Ten Boom)* In Germany, they slaughtered my family, out of hate and prejudice, because we provided safety for Jews in 1943. But they forgot one thing—we were on the Lord's side.

Actor 6: They mocked me for my faith as I prayed at my high school.

Actor 7: They hated me because I wouldn't go to their parties and wouldn't laugh at their crude jokes. I wouldn't give in to their philosophy of life that wasn't in God's plan.

Actor 8: They called me a dreamer who believed in fairy tales from a 2000-year-old book. But they forgot one thing—I was on the Lord's side.

Actor 1: They sought to destroy me. . .

Actor 2: To beat me. . .

Actor 3: To kill my child. . .

Actor 4: To wipe out a whole nation. . .

Actor 5: To defeat our dream. . .

Actor 5,6, & 7: To mock our belief in Jesus. . .

Actor 3: But they forgot one thing. . .

All: We were on the Lord's side.

~

GOD IS LOVE
by Jason & Michelle Strickland

A creative reading that's great for Sunday morning

Adapted from: *1 John 4: 7a, 8, 16, and 1 Corinthians 1-8, and 13.*

Purpose: *To show that since God is love, all of the attributes that describe love describe God.*

Cast: *Three Readers*

Reader 1: Dear friends,

Reader 2: let us love one another,

Reader 3: for love comes from God.

Reader 1: Whoever does not love, does not know God, because God is love.

Reader 2: And so we know and rely on the love God has for us. God is love. Whoever lives in love lives in God, and God in him.

Reader 3: If I speak in the tongues of men and of angels, but have not...

Reader 1: God...

Reader 3: ...I am only a resounding gong or a clanging cymbal.

Reader 1: ...is love.

Reader 2: If I have the gift of prophecy and can fathom all mysteries and all knowledge, and if I have a faith that can move mountains, but have not...

Reader 3: God...

Reader 2: ...I am nothing.

Reader 3: ...is love.

Reader 1: If I give all I possess to the poor and surrender my body to the flames, but have not...

Reader 2: God...

Reader 1: ...I gain nothing.

Reader 2: ...is love.

Reader 3: God...

Reader 1: ...is patient,

Reader 3: God...

Reader 2: ...is kind,

Reader 3: God...

Reader 1: ...does not envy,

Reader 3: God...

Reader 2: ...does not boast,

Reader 3: God...

Reader 1: ...is not proud,

Reader 2: ...is not rude,

Reader 1: ...is not self-seeking,

Reader 3: God...

Reader 2: ...is not easily angered,

Reader 1: ...keeps no record of wrongs,

Reader 2: ...does not delight in evil but rejoices with the truth,

Reader 3: God...

Reader 1: ...always protects,

Reader 2: ...always trusts,

Reader 1: ...always hopes,

Reader 2: ...always perseveres.

Reader 3: ..is love!

Reader 1: God never fails.

Reader 2: Prophecies will cease.

Reader 3: God never fails.

Reader 1: Tongues will be stilled.

Reader 2: God never fails.

Reader 3: Knowledge will pass away.

Reader 1: God never fails.

Reader 2: And now these three remain:

Reader 1: faith, hope, and love.

Reader 3: But the greatest of these is...

All: God—is love.

TO FOLLOW HIM
by Nancy Sheffey

A parable of pilgrimage

Cast: *3 actors and numerous extras*
  No Need: a fashionably well-dressed man
  No Good: a shabby, poorly attired man (this could be played by a woman)
  Christian: an actor whose voice and manner is kind, nonthreatening, and compassionate

Props: *ladder, duffle bag, rope*

Setting: *The stage is set with a tall ladder placed sideways to the audience (preferably a wooden ladder as it is heavier and will make less noise).* **No Need** *sits atop it, imperiously gazing out over the audience. He takes no heed of the action taking place beneath him. At the foot of the ladder and to the side sits* **No Good**. *A black duffle bag is behind him. Throughout the sketch, people of all ages and sizes walk across the set, alone, together, sporadically crossing the stage or platform.*

No Good watches the people going past him, studying them. Finally, he can stand it no longer and he stands and shyly stops one of the extras.

No Good: Uh—excuse me. Where are you going?

Extra #1: *(pointing forward)* That way. (*doesn't really stop but says this, continuing forward.)*

No Good: *(letting one or two go by before he tries again)* Pardon me. *(He tries to talk to two extras walking together.)* Could you tell me where you're going?

Extras #2 and **#3:** *(simultaneously, but without even slowing down)* Can't talk now, Buddy. Gotta run. Later!

Another one or two pass by, but **No Good** *refuses to give up. He reaches out and grabs* **Christian** *by the arm as he walks past and says with forceful frustration...*

No Good: Hey! Who *are* you people?

Christian: *(startled)* Why, we're Christians.

No Good: Really?

Christian: You sound surprised.

No Good: Yeah, well, I always thought...I mean, I heard that...well, you look like...like regular people!

Christian: *(laughing good-naturedly)* Well, that's what we are.

No Good: What are you all doing?

Christian: Following Jesus.

No Good: But where are you going?

Christian: Wherever the Lord leads.

No Good: Where's that?

Christian: *(patiently and with tenderness)* From where we are now—through tomorrow—into eternity.

No Good: No kidding? *(looks at the people passing)* You...you seem to have such purpose...like you're sure of where you're going.

Christian: I've been following a long time—long enough to know that God is faithful. He knows what I need—what is best for me—even when I don't. *(As he has said this, he moves to one side and **No Good** quickly moves in front of him, obviously trying to hide the duffle bag behind him.)* What is that you're hiding?

No Good: Nothing.

Christian: It's okay.

No Good: *(looking at his feet)* It's…it's my past.

Christian: Oh. *(pauses thoughtfully)* If you were to follow Jesus, you wouldn't have to worry about your past.

No Good: *(head snaps up and with surprise says)* What? *(He drops his head again quickly.)* No. You don't understand. I'm No Good. *(He says this as he would his name, with the emphasis on "no.")* I've done some awful things—

Christian: It's not what you've done that matters to Jesus. It's who you are: a person He created, whom He loves, and who needs Him.

No Good: No. He wouldn't want me. I'm not good enough.

Christian: Neither am I. *(No Good looks at him.)* Neither are they. *(Christian gestures to the followers going by and No Good looks at them.)* We could never be good enough, friend. But God loves us and wants a relationship with us.

No Good: How do you know?

Christian: Because He proved it when He died on a cross, giving His life for ours. *(He takes No Good by the arm and starts to lead him forward as he continues. No Good is protesting saying, "I can't!" "I can't follow!" but Christian keeps talking.)* Come with me and I'll introduce you. You can leave your past behind and just. . .

Christian has stopped because he realizes No Good is not with him, but behind him, and we see he is tethered to the duffle bag, a rope around his waist hidden by his T-shirt, and he stands at the end of the rope. Christian looks back at him in surprise.)

No Good: I *told* you I can't follow. I'm tied to my past.

Christian: No Good, the Bible says *(walking back to him)* if any man is in Christ, he is a new creature—the old things *(indicates the bag)* have passed away—the new has come. Jesus can make you a new creature.

No Good: *(amazed)* He—He can do that?

Christian: He did it for me, *(indicates other followers.)* for them. He wants to do it for you. Will you believe that and come with me—or stay bound?

No Good: *(looks back at his bag and then back to Christian and in a halting low voice says)* I…I never knew. *(With trembling hands he begins to untie himself as Christian rejoices—)*

Christian: Hallelujah!

This outburst startles No Need atop the ladder. He looks down for the first time.

No Need: Hey! Keep it down! *(Realizes his pun.)* Ha! Ha! *(Says it again to himself.)* Keep it down…hey…hey *(Chuckling—he is his own greatest fan—then looks down again.)* No pun intended.

No Good: *(to Christian)* That's No Need.

Christian: *(to No Need)* What are you doing up there?

No Need: Living the high life—what does it look like?

Christian: How'd you get up there?

No Need: Climbed. Over everything and everybody it took to get here. And I did it alone. I'm a self-made man. What I need, I buy—what I want, I take. I'm master of my destiny. *(looking out over the audience)* King of my domain. *(looking back down at them)* You a friend of No Good?

Christian: Yes.

No Good: *(to No Need)* He's a follower of Christ. All of these people are followers.

No Need: *(unimpressed)* Really? I didn't notice. I rarely look down.

No Good: This guy says Christ can change your life—give it purpose and meaning.

No Need: My purpose—money, the meaning—position. I have both.

Christian: But deep inside there's an emptiness, isn't there? *(He starts up the ladder. No Need begins to protest but Christian keeps coming, talking in a voice that is sure and steady.)* It gnaws at you at night—whenever you're alone. So you try not to be alone. *(No Need is losing his composure as Christian accurately describes his condition.)* You fill your days and nights with more people, more places, more things, thinking that the next thing you get will satisfy—but it never does. The hole is still there. You still feel incomplete because what you need you can't take or buy...*(He is face-to-face with No Need.)* What you need is Jesus.

No Need: *(in a hoarse whisper)* Who...who *are* you?

Christian: Someone who knows, my friend. *(looks around at the view)* I used to have this view. *(looks back at No Need)* I used to have that feeling, but there's nothing that satisfies, No Need. Nothing, but Jesus. Why don't you come with us? I'll introduce you to Him—He's the answer to the emptiness. *(coaxes him)* Come on. *(Christian starts down then looks up to see No Need clutching the top of the ladder, unmoving, watching him. In a voice patient and understanding...)* You've got to come down to follow.

No Need begins to climb down. Christian has gotten to the floor, beside an amazed No Good, who says in low voice so as not to be heard by No Need...

No Good: How did you do that?

Christian: Told him what I told you. The truth. And the truth will set you free.

No Good: But how'd you know he felt like that? I never would've guessed it! All this time, I've been so jealous of him, big guy like that, the man who's got it all.

Christian: He is as bound as you. Tied to things, wealth, position. But like you, Jesus can take care of all that.

No Need has made it to the ground, looks sheepishly at No Good.

No Need: You going, No Good?

No Good: Yeah.

Christian: *(putting his arms around their shoulders)* Well, let's go. *(They start off with the other followers and lights dim out as Christian says...)* The first thing we gotta do is get you guys some new names!

PRAYER
by Scott Icenhower

If prayer is so simple, why don't we pray?

Cast: *Four male Puppets: Abner, Bill, Clyde, Dave, Off Stage Voice*

Setting: *Four puppets are in a car at a fast food drive-through. A large piece of cardboard should be cut out in the shape of a car with the window area cut out wide enough for all four puppets to be seen. During the skit, the puppets, with the car cut-out, will move across the stage.*

Abner: OK, guys, the tradition continues. We finish church and then head out to the Burger Barn.

Bill: And it is about time, too. I can't believe we sang all four stanzas of that hymn. Whatever happened to *(tries to mock an old man)* "Let's just sing the first and last verses this time?"

Clyde: Yeah, my stomach was growling in church tonight.

Dave: That was your stomach? I just thought you couldn't sing.

All start laughing and punching each other.

Off Stage Voice: Welcome to Burger Barn. May I take your order?

Abner: *(startled)* Oh yeah, uh—hey, what do you guys want?

Bill: Two cheeseburgers, fries, and a Coke.

Abner: *(turning toward speaker)* Two cheeseburgers, fries, and a Coke.

Clyde: Burger Barn Big-Boy, fries, and a Coke.

Abner: *(turning back toward speaker)* Burger Barn Big-Boy, fries, and a coke—make that three. Hey, what do you want?

Bill: Hummmm, I'll have a double bacon Monster-Mac on wheat, hold the onions and mayo, but go heavy on the ketchup—oh, and cook it medium well.

Abner: *(hesitates, then turns to speaker)* I hope you heard all of that.

Off Stage Voice: Sure did, but it takes a little longer to fix the special order. Would you pull over to our waiting area?

Abner: Okay.

The group moves over to the opposite side of the stage.

Abner: *(looking at Bill)* Man, you always do this to us. Why do you have to ask for weird things?

Clyde: Ask and it shall be given you. That's what the preacher was talking about tonight. You know, prayer—asking God for stuff. It's just like the drive-through. You go to a particular place, speak out loud—asking God for something—and bingo!

Dave: Your stomach must have growled so loud you couldn't hear the preacher. Prayer is more than just asking God for stuff.

Abner: Of course. A lot of times I thank Him for all that He's done for me.

Bill: And there are times when I tell Him how much I love Him.

Dave: You see? Prayer is talking to God, not giving Him your order. Sometimes you might ask Him for something, but you have to ask according to His will.

Abner: Yeah, and you can pray anywhere, any time.

Bill: Hey guys, here comes our food. Clyde, do you want to say the blessing?

Clyde: I sure do. *(all heads bow)*

COLD FOOD OR COLD HEART
by Rick Shoemaker

Cast: *Adult, Child or Teen, or good for Puppets*

Props: *Table, two chairs, plates, food (can pantomime)*

Setting: *Adult and Child sit at table. Child grabs his plate and starts to fill it.*

Adult: Aren't you forgetting something?

Child: Forgetting something?

Adult: *(folds his hands as if in prayer)*

Child: *(looks at his hands)* Oh, I already washed my hands, Dad.

Adult: No. Aren't we forgetting to thank our Lord for such a bountiful feast?

Child: Oh, sure. Okay, let's pray. I'm hungry.

Adult: Son, you can lead us in prayer.

Child: *(bows his head)* God is neat. Now let's eat!

Adult: Hold on. "God is neat; now let's eat?"

Child: I told you, I'm hungry.

Adult: Maybe I should return thanks. *(bows his head)* Dear Lord, I want to take a few moments to thank You for this fine meal. Thank You for the chicken who laid these eggs; and for the pig who gave his life for this bacon that smells so good; and for the cow that gave this good milk; and for the trees that grew the fruit for this juice; and for the wheat that gave us the flour for these biscuits. I really appreciate it.

Lord, thanks for the farmers who work so hard to raise the chickens, and pigs, and cows. Bless those hard-working people. And for the people in the grocery stores who help keep the food fresh and available, bless them. I don't recall ever thanking You for my refrigerator. I don't like warm milk, and this old refrigerator has been a good one over the years to keep my milk nice and cold. And to keep all that food from getting spoiled. Thank You for the assembly line workers who made my refrigerator and my stove. Raw eggs wouldn't be nearly as good as cooked ones! And I guess I ought to ask You to bless the gas and electric company workers. The refrigerator and the stove wouldn't be much good without those people. I know I tend to complain a little when I pay the bill each month, but bless them, anyway, Lord.

Come to think of it, I want to thank You for my job. I've been unemployed before and You helped us get by. But having a regular income sure is fine. And Lord, I want to thank You for my nose. That bacon sure does smell good! Smelling it is almost as good as eating it! Speaking of that, I want to thank You for my teeth. This food wouldn't do me much good without my teeth. Now Grandpa does a pretty good job of gumming his meals, but I just want to thank You that I can still chomp mine.

And I want to thank You that I'm not eating alone. It's good to have my son with me. I don't like eating alone. I want You to know my boy didn't mean no disrespect by his praying. At least, I don't think so. Anyway, Lord, thank You again for this meal. Amen.

Child: I thought you'd never finish! The food is gonna get cold!

Adult: Son, better to have cold food than cold hearts!

~

REACHING THE PEAK
by Matt Tullos

These five scenes can be used in a number of ways and in a number of settings. They can be read during Bible studies, or performed as a series of vignettes during several worship services. The collection forms a parable which alludes to the Christian journey as a mountainous adventure full of breathtaking summits, dangerous caverns, and tempting alternate routes! Feel free to mold the concepts within this allegory to fit your needs!

Cast:

J.C.: Journey guide up the Mountain of Happiness

Luci: Journey guide into D. Valley

David: Mountain hiker

Cari: Mountain hiker

John: Mountain hiker

Kevin: Valley dweller

Valerie: Valley dweller

Leslie: Valley dweller

Madge: Valley dweller

Rupert: Valley dweller

THE INVITATION

The choice is yours!

Cari: *(walks in, looking at a map)* This is where we're supposed to meet. I must be early, or maybe they printed this map upside down. Anybody around?

Kevin, David, and Madge enter—singing a hiking or camping song. (They see Cari.)

Kevin: This must be the spot.. *(to Cari)* Are you here for the Journey?

Cari: I'm relieved. I thought I might have been late.

Valerie: *(enters from the other side, looking at her watch)* No, we're all early.

David: *(to Cari)* So you're not the tour guide.

Cari: I'm afraid not.

Madge: I think Dr. Seuss wrote the invitation. *(she reads)* "Welcome to the opportunity of a lifetime. It's absolutely free, but as you will see, it will only cost your life."

Kevin: *(reading)* "This call is for all."

Madge: "Accepted by many, accepted by some...Whosoever will, may come." *(end of invitation)*

Leslie and Rupert wander in.

Cari: This is different from most explorations. Did you notice that we have a choice?

David: Mountain of Happiness or D. Valley.

Rupert: Oh, Sweetheart, wherever you want to go.

Leslie: No, I want you to make the decision. Just let me dwell in your shadow.

Madge: I may throw up.

Leslie: If you asked me to, I'd follow you anywhere.

Rupert: Every breath you take, I'll be watching you.

David: I don't know if this is "American Top 40" or "The Love Connection!"

Leslie and Rupert pay no attention as they whisper sweet nothings to each other, totally engrossed in their relationship.

Kevin: Is D. Valley like a...Jamaican valley? Com' to de valley...It's de place to be, mon.

Madge: It's D with a period behind it.

Rupert: Sounds mysterious.

Leslie: Alluring.

Rupert: Romantic.

Leslie: As in dimly lit—

Rupert: As in deserted.

Leslie: As in desire.

Rupert: As in dreamy.

Valerie: As in disgusting! Will you two cut it out!

Luci enters. She is wearing an outfit that gives her the look of a hiking expert. She's confident. As she enters, it becomes obvious that she's a leader.

Luci: Good morning, friends. I'm glad to see that you're on time. Let me take a second to check the sign-up list. David?

David: Here.

Luci: Kevin?

Kevin: Yo!

Luci: Valerie?

Valerie: Present.

Luci: Leslie and Rupert?

Leslie and **Rupert:** *(together)* We're here! *(The rest of them groan.)*

Luci: Madge?

Madge: Here.

Luci: Cari?

Cari: Over here.

Luci: John? *(waits a beat)* Oh John?

John enters hurriedly.

John: Excuse me. I'm supposed to go on this trip. Like—an incredible mountain hike. And I think I'm gonna be late.

Luci: You're just in time.

John: That's the problem. By the time I find these guys they might leave without me. Have you seen a group of like—people.

Cari: What do we look like?

John: Like a group of... *(realization hits)*...cool!

Luci: You must be John.

John: Excellent.

Luci: Cari?

Cari: Over here.

Luci: Wonderful. Everyone's present and accounted for. Let me welcome you to Journeys Unlimited. I'm sure you've read all the information about this incredible Journey. It'll be one that you'll never forget. Not in a million years. As you probably know, you have a decision to make; the low road to D. Valley or the high road to the Mountain of Happiness. Let me describe the two.

Madge: What does the "D" stand for?

Luci: I believe it means dynamic and delightful. That's for you to decide. Let me first say that I am the tour guide for D. Valley. D. Valley is a place of great pleasure. There are a million things to do and see. The path is as wide as you want it to be. And as your guide, I'm here to help you see all the possibilities. If it's freedom you want, then this is the way to go.

Kevin: Definitely sounds delightful!

Luci: You're catching on quick.

Cari: What about the Mountain of Happiness?

Luci: It's been a long time since I've been there. I used to live on the Mountain, but not any more. The Valley is my kind of place.

David: I bet the view is breathtaking!

Luci: Perhaps it is. But the trail is very narrow and it's up hill all the way. It's a long, sweaty hike.

Rupert and **Leslie:** Eeew...yuk!

Luci: I'm sure you've been thinking about which direction you'd like to go—so let's vote. All in favor of the D. Valley, raise your hand. (*Luci scans the group. All hands except David's, John's, Cari's are raised.*) Wonderful! Almost everyone. And as for those wanting to go up the mountain? (*David and Cari timidly raise their hands. John raises his hand wildly.*) Are you sure you want to go through with this? It's uphill all the way.

Cari: I can't explain exactly why, but I've been in valleys before, and I've heard that the climb is worth it.

David: I have, too.

John: Ditto.

Luci: All right, then, if that's your choice.

David: You said that you don't travel the Mountain path anymore. Do we have a guide?

Luci: You do. His name is J.C.

Cari: Where is He?

Luci: I haven't seen J.C. in years. I don't even know if He exists. Some climbers seem certain that He does. But it's a gamble. Excuse me, friends, let me get these people squared away, and then let the party begin. (*to David and Cari*) Are you sure you want to do this? Hiking down is much easier than hiking up.

David: I want to go up. I've got my heart set on the peak.

Luci: Well, there's the trail—but before you go, let me give you the essentials for your attempted climb. (*She pulls out a bag of equipment.*) First of all, you need a book of rules. Don't leave until you've memorized it. You'll need a tent to shelter you. You'll need this. (*She pulls out a shotgun.*)

David: A shotgun? What for?

Luci: Lions and tigers and bears.

Cari: Oh my!

Luci: It would be good for you to read these. (*She pulls out a stack of books and gives some to David and Cari.*)

David: More books?

Cari: (*reading the title of one*) "Famous Tragedies of Mountain Climbers."

David: "One Hundred and One Things Not to Do on the Mountain of Happiness."

Luci: Just a few more things to think about...and a gallon of water a piece.

Cari: How are we supposed to carry all of this stuff?!

Luci: Frankly, I don't know. But they're all very essential.

Kevin: Are you sure you don't want to come with us?

Cari and David look at each other undecidedly, then...

David: Yes, I'm sure. I don't know why, but I need to climb.

Cari: Maybe we'll get lucky and make it to the top.

Luci: Don't count on it, Girl. By the way, that map that you were given by the mountain climbers...I wouldn't put too much faith in it. It's never been proven to be accurate. (*to the valley dwellers*) Well, we'd better get going. The Valley is beckoning us.

Rupert: (*still dumbstruck by Leslie*) How romantic!

Valerie groans.

Madge: Do we need anything for our journey?

Luci: Not now. You've got me. What more do you need?

Valerie: So all we have to do is follow you?

Luci: If you like. If not, just remember—if you're going down, you're on the right path. We'll meet eventually. And so without any further delay—to the Valley!

All Valley Dwellers: To the Valley!

David, John, and Cari are left alone on stage as the valley dwellers exit.

David: I hope we're doing the right thing.

Cari: It certainly wasn't the popular thing.

John: How are we supposed to carry all this stuff?

Cari: Beats me.

David: Why don't you load us down, and you carry what's left?

Cari: Sounds like a good idea. *(She surveys the pile of stuff.)* Well, let's see ...Luci said we didn't need the map. The books are the heaviest things *(She tries to load stuff into David's arms.)* And the water jugs...

John: *(loaded down)* This is nuts! We haven't even started, and I'm already floored!

Cari: There's got to be an easier way.

David: Where's our journey guide? What was His name?

Cari: I think she said His name was J.C.

J.C.: Did you call me?

John: Whoa!! You must be J.C.?

J.C.: Yes. As a matter of fact, I am.

David: Boy, are we glad to see you! How are we supposed to carry all these things? First, there's the water and the books. Then you've got the shotgun and the tent. Then you add—

J.C.: Luci's been up to her old tricks again.

Cari: Her old tricks?

J.C.: You don't need any of that. All you need is the map.

David: The map is the one thing she said we didn't need.

J.C.: Sure, there are those on the journey upward who bring a lot of equipment. Stuff that they think will get them to the peak, but all they ever need is the map. *(looking at the water jugs)* And why carry your water with you when your map can guide you to wells?

David: The tent. We've got to bring our tents.

J.C.: The map will show you lodging. Sure you can bring tons of excess baggage, but it'll only slow you down. All you need is the map, each other, and Me. You didn't make the easy choice when you chose the high road to Happiness, but you did make the right choice. Support each other, and rely on My wisdom, and you'll go higher than you've ever dreamed.

Cari: So, how do I start?

J.C.: Drop all your things and follow.

David: That's it?

J.C.: That's it.

Cari: Well, what are we waiting for! Let's go!

~

THE TRAIL RULES
Based on the Beatitudes
Advice from the guides

Luci and J.C. enter the room in hiking attire. They speak directly to the audience. They are making separate presentations and don't acknowledge each other's presence. Groups may want to have the climbers with J.C. on stage and the Valley dwellers with Luci. If that is done, you will want to have the rules directed toward them. You may want to add questions from the valley dwellers and the mountain climbers. In any case, keep them separate—to give them a feeling of being in two entirely separate locations.

Luci: OK, folks. I know that you're anxious to get to D.Valley, so let's talk about a strategy.

J.C.: Strategy is crucial on this trip, so on the map see the—

Luci: —list of these rules which shouldn't be hard to follow at all. Just do what comes naturally!

J.C.: You'll find the rules very challenging. It won't come naturally at all. But remember the goal. The peak is incredible! And it's the only way to life.

Luci: It's the only way to fulfill all your forbidden desires. The first rule is— Realize that you have all the answers on your own. You're #1. And don't forget it!

J.C.: The first rule on the High Road to Happiness is that you can't climb the mountain by yourself. You have to realize that without my help you are poor. No one with a proud heart can make it up the mountain without falling.

Luci: Rule #2—Party-Hardy!! Eat drink and be merry! Live it up. Tomorrow you may die!

J.C.: Realize who you are. I've been waiting for you to start this journey. You didn't believe that it was real. Or at least you didn't want to climb. Maybe out of laziness, or selfishness, you simply ignored My invitation. If you regret those years of wandering, then you've fulfilled the second rule. Grief over the past, over the lost years of wandering.

Luci: Don't plan for the future. And don't repent over the past. Don't turn around and try to start up the mountain!

J.C.: That brings us to Rule #3—Don't flaunt your strength as a climber. Control your strength. Many climbers have fallen off the cliffs of the High Road because they placed too much confidence in themselves.

Luci: Rule #3—If you've got it, flaunt it. Talk trash. Let everybody know who you are. If you seem confident, chances are you can get what you want in D. Valley. Have fun but don't let anybody push you around. And then there's—

J.C.: Rule #4—Seek to learn as much as you can about the trail. Follow the signs. Look for the warning signs in the map.

Luci: Rule #4—Relax, don't pay attention to the warning signs. Most of the warning signs only apply to the climbers, not the valley dwellers. Which brings us to Rule #5—You deserve every right that you can possibly have. And if someone slaps you, then if I were you, I'd slap them right back!

J.C.: Rule #5—If you see any climbers who've fallen, lost their footing or just plain blown it, you must stop to help them. I don't care how much time you lose. Getting to the peak isn't all there is. It's who you help along the way. And Rule #6 goes along with it. It says that you must climb with a pure heart. Let me put it this way. You have to keep your eyes on the peak.   Feel free to rest for a while. It's important to rest, but don't find a house with a nice view of the valley and retire.

Luci: Rule #6—Keep having fun. And take your time. Don't walk a straight line. I prefer the circular motion myself. And I think you will, too.

J.C.: Rule #7- Don't fight with anyone. Climbers who fight usually end up rolling down the hill.

Luci: Rule #7—If you want to survive in the Valley, then you're going to have to learn how to fight. And if they gang up on you, find your own gang and have at it. That's Rule #8.

J.C.: If the valley dwellers ambush you, be happy. Rejoice! It will make the accomplishment of your peak performance that much more satisfying.   If you run into any problems, I'll be here. You don't need a cellular telephone or a bull horn. I'm with you. All you have to do is ask.

HERE FOR YOU

Luci visits the High Road

Cari, David and John enter. They are weary from a full morning of climbing. They sit down to rest, massage their feet, and drink from a canteen.

David: Finally! Some level ground. My feet are killing me.

Cari: I think I've developed a blister on my little toe!

John: *(in baby talk)* Poor whittle baby! Does she have a whittle boo-boo on her whittle toe?

David: Give her a break, John!

Cari: Sticks and stones may break my bones but baby talk will never harm me.

John: I forgot. You're a girl. Just another indication of the superior nature of men.

Cari: Now hold on one second! It seems to me that you left two hours earlier than we did and you'd still be in that mud pit if we hadn't pulled you out. How many times do we have to go over the rules with you! Don't leave without checking in with J.C. every day.

John: First of all, it's a stupid rule.

David: Stupid?

John: Sure! J.C. knows where I am. he doesn't need me to check in everyday. I keep up with him at least once a week. If he needs me to do something, I figure that he'll call.

Cari: John, you're not even listening! Checking in with J.C. isn't mainly for his sake. It's for your

sake! He warned us before we ever hit the trail this morning that there was a mud pit.

David: A mud pit so thick it would be impossible to get out of it alone.

John: Don't remind me.

Cari: It seems like we have to constantly remind you.

John: *(almost angry)* Well then go ahead. Leave me here if I'm that much trouble.

Cari: Don't believe that we haven't ever thought of it. But J.C. said we have to stay together if we're going to make it to the peak.

Luci enters.

Luci: Hi! How are things on the way up?

David: Hey Luci. What are you doing up here? I thought you were in D. Valley.

Luci: That's where I live, but I like coming up here and checking on the mountain climbers as much as I can. Looks like you've had a rough day. Hard climb?

Cari: One of the more difficult days.

Luci: Well, I know that you've made a commitment to climb but feel free to slide on down and visit us in the Valley! You might even want to rent a room and live it up for a while. You could just cut loose! Work off some steam! Relax.

John: You mean we could just go back to D. Valley? Just like that?

Luci: It's as easy as falling into a ditch.

John: I can certainly do that.

David: You can say that again!

Luci: Sounds like you might be interested, John.

John: D. Valley—I never did get to see it.

Luci: You can't be an official citizen, but nobody cares. We've got lots of climbers who've been down in D. Valley for years.

John: Sounds like I can't lose.

Cari: No way! You are not going down there! *(She grabs John's arm.)*

David: She's right, John. We're a team. You've made a commitment.

John: *(long cerebral pause)* I'm going.

Luci: Great.

David: What!?

Cari: I don't believe it! What about J.C.? What about us?

John: Sorry guys. I'll come back up sometime.

Cari: *(to Luci)* You can't do this. You can't just pull him away like this!

Luci: Watch me.

Luci and John exit. As David speaks, J.C. enters.

David: He's always been a bit inconsistent in his climbing, but I never thought he. . .

J.C.: Don't be surprised. It happens all the time.

Cari: J.C.! You're just in time! Luci is taking John to—

J.C.: To D. Valley.

Cari: Well what are you waiting for? Aren't you going down there to get him.

J.C.: I can't.

David: Now wait a minute. I've seen you do some incredible things on the path to the peak. This will be a piece of cake.

J.C.: No. You don't understand. He has a free will. If I forced him to stay on the High Road, he wouldn't be a climber at all. He'd be my slave. I give you the freedom to climb. I won't carry you kicking and screaming to the peak.

Cari: Will he come back?

J.C. is silent.

David: That's another one of those questions that you won't answer.

J.C.: Precisely. Many climbers go and spend their lives in D. Valley. They totally forget about the peak and my invitation. But when the allotted tour time is completed they regret every moment that they spent there. I wish they could see D. Valley for what it is.

Cari: And what is it?

J.C.: What do you think?

David: Death Valley.

J.C.: You're catching on, David. There's still plenty of light. Keep climbing. Call on me. I'm here for you.

Interpretive movement possibility—"Here for You" recorded by Michael W. Smith.

THE MOUNTAIN WALL
Evaluating Your Attitudes

The most difficult walls to conquer are the man-made ones

David and J.C. enter alone in hiking gear.

David: I thought you said it would be best if I stayed with other climbers.

J.C.: You'll be back with them in a little while. It's very important that you travel with other climbers, but there are parts of this mountain that you have to travel alone.

David: Well, I'll do it, but I don't like it.

J.C.: Sorry, David.

David: Besides, this part of the journey doesn't look difficult at all. The trail is wide and there doesn't seem to be too much of an incline.

J.C.: Some of the biggest obstacles on the High Road to Happiness can't be—

At this very moment, David runs into an invisible wall. Then falls down.

J.C.: —seen.

David: What was that!? I hit something.

J.C.: Don't say that I didn't warn you.

David: Not much of a warning, that's for sure.

J.C: Some lessons are better experienced than taught.

J.C. walks across the area where David was knocked down.

David: How did you do that?

J.C.: Do what?

David: Walk through that wall?

J.C.: Simple.

David: Simple?

J.C.: That's your wall, not mine.

David: Now hold on a second. Walls don't just apply to certain people. A wall can't decide who it belongs to. Can it?

J.C.: Not on any ordinary journey, but this is no ordinary journey.

David: You can say that again.

J.C.: This is no ordinary journey.

David: Very funny.

J.C.: I couldn't resist.

David: Can I climb over it?

J.C.: From the looks of it, no.

David: How come you can see it and I can't?

J.C.: I'm your guide. You have to trust me.

David: What does it look like?

J.C.: It's not a very attractive wall at all. Looks like it's been around for years.

David: What's it made of?

J.C.: Attitudes.

David: You mean to tell me that I just ran smack dab into my attitudes?

J.C.: You're catching on.

David: This is weird.

J.C.: No it's not weird. It may be ugly but it is normal. Over to the left is pride. More to the right is anger over the past; and way up at the top is rebelliousness. And... well, I could go on and on. Most climbers run into an attitude wall and give up. They spend half their lives trying to scale it but it's an impossible task.

David: If I can't climb it, what do I have to do?

J.C.: It's very simple. Turn your back to the wall.

David: You want me to walk down the mountain?

J.C.: Don't get ahead of me! Do you really think I'd want you to do that? Don't walk. Just turn your back to the wall.

David obeys.

David: OK. What next?

J.C.: Fall backwards.

David: Fall backwards? Is this some kind of joke? I could break my neck! I'm still hurting from a few minutes ago. And now you want me to fall backwards onto the wall? You know what would hit the wall first, don't you?

J.C.: Your head.

David: Exactly.

J.C.: Exactly. David, listen close. I know this sounds illogical. That's why so many climbers never make it over their attitude wall. But you've got to trust me. Fall backwards. The force of your fall will make contact with what you trust the most. If you rely on your own attitudes and strengths, then you'll hit the wall. Not a pleasant experience, I agree. If you have more trust in me than the wall, then the wall will cease to exist and I'll break your fall. No harm. No foul.

David: Couldn't I just walk through it? Could I wear a helmet?

J.C.: David. Trust me.

David: Could I fall forward?

J.C.: David!

David: OK.

With much hesitancy, David turns around, falls backwards, and J.C. breaks the fall.

David: Wow! I did it!

J.C.: Of course.

David stands up and runs through the area where the wall used to be.

David: How did that happen? The wall! Where did it go?

J.C.: What wall?

REACHING THE PEAK
A concluding invitation to the High Road

Peak performance is an adventure!

On the stage is a sign reading—"Peak of Understanding." As David and Cari enter, they are looking around in awe.

David: Wow! What a view!

Cari: It's so peaceful.

David: Look over there! Across the meadow—

Cari: What about it?

David: Don't you recognize it? The Forest of Confusion.

Cari: Oh, I see it now.

David: I'm glad I'm here and not there.

Cari: I've never seen so many traps and thistles in my entire life.

David: It was strange to see hikers living in a place that was so uh...

Cari: Confusing?

David: Right!

Cari: Did you notice all the streets just off the narrow path to the peak? They went in every possible direction but they all merged into a giant expressway to D. Valley.

J.C. enters unnoticed.

David: Everything seems so clear now. I wish I could stay here forever.

J.C.: But you can't. The kingdom moves forward and upward.

Cari: Hey! Where did you come from.

J.C.: You should know me well enough to know that I wasn't far away.

David: So how did we do?

J.C.: You've done great so far. You've stayed on the path. That's the important part. And you've followed my lead.

David: And we've stayed together.

Cari: Could I ask a question?

J.C.: That's why I'm here.

Cari: Here we are at the Peak of Understanding. Right?

J.C.: Right.

Cari: We can see where we've been, but we can't see where we're going. Don't you think we'd be better prepared if—

J.C.: —if you could see what's ahead? *(knowing laugh)* Cari, remember that it's not a journey by sight. It's a journey by trust. Do you trust me?

Cari: I'd like to think that I do—

J.C.: I will give you enough vision for the day. No more... no less... Now—I have a surprise for you. An old friend. (*John walks in covered with dirt. Cari laughs.*)

John: Go ahead, enjoy yourself, Cari.

Cari: What happened?

John: What didn't happen! I found out what D. Valley means. Dirt valley.

J.C.: Actually it means death.

John: That too! I thought I was going to die! After a few days down there you begin to realize that the whole place just stinks. Everyone wears masks to cover up the dirt and heavy cologne to cover up their body odor. They seemed to be having fun, but every party I went to left me feeling, well, out of place.

J.C.: Most climbers in D. Valley aren't very happy after they've seen the peak... if they've seen the peak.

John: So I decided to come back to the path.

J.C.: Clean yourself up. You've got some climbing to do. You look a bit out of shape. There's a stream just around the bend.

They talk as they exit.

David: I hope you still have some soap; you look awful.

John: You should have seen the other guys down there! They had an odor that could kill a horse! And they didn't even know it—

Still talking improvisationally as they leave.

J.C.: And so the journey continues. What about you? Will you follow one of the million paths that leads to Death Valley or will you travel the High Road to Happiness? Who will join us? It's not the easy decision. It's a difficult climb. It's not the choice of your generation. Most of your friends have already chosen to fly down the road to the valley. But ultimately it's a road of destruction. I wish they could see it. I wish they knew that I'd lead them away from death into everlasting life! Perhaps they don't want to believe or maybe nobody's told them about the peak. (*transitional pause*) Well, I have to be going. If you want to climb the peak, just call on me. I'll hear from you.

Off-Stage Voice: Hey! J.C.! I'm stuck!

J.C.: (*to off-stage voice*) I'll be right there! (*to audience*) Sounds like somebody's stuck in the materialism mud hole again. Life goes onward. I just hope you go upward!

~

CELEBRATING SEX IN YOUR MARRIAGE

by Matt and Darlene Tullos

Here is a collection of scripts designed for the married adult audience. Try using these scripts at your next married adult banquet, conference, or retreat. Most are in readers theatre format, so they are very easy to use!

DON'T SAY THAT WORD!

An overview of the "S" word in the Bible

He: And God created man

She: male *(pointing to him)*

He: and female *(pointing to her)*

Both: He created them.

She: In His own image.

He: God knew that man shouldn't be alone.

She: So He created woman.

Both: Unity, oneness, purpose, fulfillment.

He: And God created sex.

She gasps.

He: What's the big deal?

She: You said it!

He: Said what? Sex?

She: Can you at least keep your voice down?

He: Why? There aren't any kids out there. This is a marriage retreat. It's not a family conference. I can say sex as loud as I want to! Don't you even know what the theme is?

She: Yes I know. You don't have to say it.

He: "Celebrating Sex in Your Marriage."

She: I said you didn't have to say it!

He: What's wrong with you! We drive hours upon end to perform drama for the marriage retreat, and I can't even say the theme?

She: Somebody might hear you.

He: Hear what?

She: Hear you say. . .

He: Yes?

She: You know-

He: Sex?

She: There you go again.

He: You are a perfect example of the terrible misconception of sex in the life of a Christian.

She: Could you maybe just say "it" when you refer to. . .

He: To what?

She: *(under her breath)* Sex.

He: Did you hear that, folks!? She said sex!

She: You don't have to make a big deal out of it.

He: It took her a while.

She: Matt!

He: But she said it!

She: Will you stop it!

He: Some of you in the back might not have heard her, but she did it! She said it!

She: It's not that I can't say it. I'm just a bit embarrassed with the word.

He: What word?

She: Sex.

He: She said it again! Two times in one year!

She: Look, this is going to be a long night if you—

He: OK, I know you're uncomfortable with saying the word "sex." That's fine. But we've got a job to do tonight and somebody's got to say it.

She: Say what?

He: Sex.

She: Oh yeah.

He: I'll say sex for you if you really feel uncomfortable with it. Tonight and tonight only! *(with "Gone with the Wind" flare)* But Scarlett, tomorrow is another day.

She: OK, Rhett.

He: Sex itself is a celebration!

She: A celebration of marriage.

He: It has been misinterpreted

She: abused

He: hidden

She: and feared.

He: But despite what man has done with this incredible gift,

She: no one can doubt that God created... *(clears throat)*

He: sex.

She: The Bible is filled with illustrations, parables, and teachings on...

He: sex.

She: God has created nations through this miraculous gift called...

He: sex.

She: Men and women, on the other hand, have used...

He: sex

She: to manipulate, control or destroy nations.

He: Nations?

She: Sure. Think about it. Sodom and Gomorrah, not to be confused with Simon and Garfunkel, perverted God's gift of...

He: sex.

She: Samson was controlled by a deceitful woman. It could be argued that lust for...

He: sex

She: ultimately led to his downfall. Then there was David.

He: Who could forget David?

She: Big mistake.

He: Very big.

She: Such a great man, and yet in a single glance he allowed his desire for...

He: sex

She: to control his life and destroy the life of a trusted officer.

He: I've got a problem with your whole approach to this issue. Is the negative all you can think about? God created men and women sexual beings. He didn't do it to frustrate us or to cause us to mess up! He created sex for our pleasure. He made it to draw the husband and wife into a sacred intimacy. Bone of my bone, flesh of my flesh.

She: Whatever that means.

He: It's about oneness, deep love, and all out exhilarating—uh—

She: —passion.

He: Right. But don't say it so loud.

She: I like the word.

He: She doesn't like the word sex, but she loves the word "passion"?

She: Anyway—you were talking about oneness.

He: Oh yeah—the Bible is a storehouse of romance! Jacob worked for years to marry Rachel. He thought he married her but when he woke up the next morning he realized that it was Leah.

She: How in the world did that happen?

He: Dark tent, I guess. The Bible says that Leah had weak eyes.

She: She wasn't the only one!

He: Back to the story. Jacob worked seven more years for Rachel! What a love!

She: How romantic!

He: And what about the story of Hosea? His love was unstoppable, unconditional. He loved Gomer in spite of her infidelity.

She: Shazzam!

He: And who could forget the love poetry of the Bible:

(with over dramatized flair)

Your hair is like a flock of goats
going down Mount Gilead.
Your teeth are like a flock of shorn sheep.
Your neck is like the tower of David.

She: I don't know whether to kiss you or slap you.

He: It loses a lot in the translation.

She: In that case—*(They kiss—just a little peck, of course.)*

He: Wow! Can we just go directly to the workshop?

She: Not yet, Honey Bear.

He: I love it when she calls me that. I feel like such a man.

She: Well, it loses a lot in the translation too!

He: I think what I'm trying to say is that sex is worth celebrating. It's from God. And every good and perfect gift is from above

She: Coming down from the Father of lights

He: With whom there is no shifting shadow.

She: He gave us a gift

He: that will unite us

She: fulfill us

He: rejuvenate us

She: inspire us

He: rekindle us

She: and thrill us.

He: Behold you are fair, my love! Behold you are fair.

> You have ravished my heart
>   with one look of your eyes,
>   with one link of your necklace.
> How fair is your love.
> How sweeter than fruit is your love.
> And the scent of your perfumes
>   than all the spices.
> Your lips, oh my spouse,
>   drip as honeycomb.
> Let my beloved come away.

She: *(knowing smile)* Let's get these workshops over with. I've got some other plans for you before the night's over.

He and She begin to briskly walk off stage. He stops her.

He: I'll catch up with you.

She: Don't keep me waiting.

As She leaves, He whispers to the audience.

He: Guys—that's Song of Solomon—Chapter 4, if you're taking notes.

THE DESIGNATED NIGHT

Sometimes even planning doesn't help!

He: Before I was married I used to think, "What a great concept!" We can sleep in the same bed, be together every night and have sex any time we want. Boy, did I have a lesson to learn!

She: We wanted to be together more, but now, with two kids, life is a little more complicated.

He: So we decided to have a designated night where we would make an effort—

She: —a valiant effort—

He: —to be together.

She: It had been so long that I decided to re-read *Intended for Pleasure* to freshen up!

Break to scene. **He** and **She** *are seated on couch.*

She: I just put the baby down. She should sleep for several hours.

He: And the dishes are done.

They are about to kiss. Before their lips meet, they are interrupted.

He: Sounds like Joey. Let me go see about him. Don't move, my love. I'll be right back. *(He exits as you hear his side of the conversation.)* We've already read your five books! *(pause)* I didn't skip any pages *(pause)* OK, I might have skipped that one. *(pause)* I'm not going to read the whole book over again! *(pause)* OK, I'll read that page and then it's lights out, Buddy! *(He reads through the page as fast as he can with humorous frustration.)* "And Little Red Riding Hood skipped through the woods without a worry or a care, knowing that Grandma's house was not far away and soon she was sure to be there." *Now good night!!*

He walks back to the couch.

He: Now where were we?

She: I think we were about to get passionate.

He: Now how could I forget that?

They are about to kiss but before their lips meet, the phone rings.

She: Hello... Oh hi Shelli! No. Not a thing. We're just getting your niece and nephew to bed. *(pause)* They're doing great! You should have heard what Joey said about you today. He was putting up his toys in the new toy box that you bought him for...(**She** *continues to mime the conversation as he speaks directly to the audience.)*

He: We'd hate to bore you with a heartfelt, long, newsy conversation between sisters, so we're going to speed up the events of the night. This conversation that my wife is having with her sister will last 44 minutes and 22 seconds, and believe you me, I'm counting every second. I could try to get her attention in various ways. *(He nuzzles her, kisses her neck, and then dances around and makes faces to get her attention, yet still is totally ignored.)* But, as you can see, she's locked in. Let's fast forward it about 44 minutes.

She hangs up the phone.

She: I'm sorry, dear, but the last time she called I was giving Christi a bath and I hate to cut her off for the second time this week.

He: You've only cut her off twice? She's better off than I am. I bet I've been cut off twice every day this week.

She: Honey, let's not fight. We can fight when the kids are awake.

They are about to kiss, but just before their lips meet they hear Joey.

He: What's the deal with him? *(very angry)* What do you want now? You just went to the bathroom an hour ago. You should be asleep! *(pause)* I don't care if you have to do number 2. Go to sleep!

She: Honey, I don't want to clean number 2 off the bed in the morning.

He: OK, Joey.

She: For the sake of time once again, we will cut directly past these adventures in the bathroom. Joey may be a bit constipated and we're almost out of time.

He: Finally! I think awhile ago I was about to kiss you.

Note: You may want to enlist someone to meow in the appropriate places.

She: Did I hear the cat?

He: No! You didn't!

They are about to kiss, but just before their lips meet...

She: That meowing is driving me crazy! He's under the table!!

He: *(delirious)* I'll teach that stupid cat a lesson! If you don't shut your trap and get out of my house, I'm going to throw you into the car and drive to Kalamazoo. Then it'll be curtains for Kitty in this household!!! *(He throws the imaginary cat out the door and tries to get control of himself.)* I can't believe this night. We planned, didn't we? *(not looking at his wife)* We did all the right things. We got the kids down early. I thought I had put out the cat. But what's worse? Hearing him meow on the inside or scrape at the window screen outside? Can't the stupid animal decide where he wants to be? And then there's Joey. He wants a book. He wants a cookie. He wants a Gummi Bear. He needs to do a number 1 and an hour later he needs to do a number 2. You know, most normal human beings do those things simultaneously! And Christi is three months old and she's still got cholera! Or was that colic? And now I'm so keyed up, I don't even know if I can think about... *(He finally sees his wife fast asleep on the couch.)* I'm glad someone's relaxed. Oh well—designated night—what an adventure!

THE PARABLE OF JENNIFER AND JERRY

Teamwork makes a difference

He: It was a monumental day in the lives of two very talented and versatile athletes: Jerry

She: and Jennifer.

He: These two athletes admired each other from afar.

She: Jerry was an expert at the 100-meter dash.

He: Jennifer was a graceful dancer who was inspired by string music and special effects.

Both: When they finally married, Jerry had a great idea.

He: I have a great idea!

She: You do?

He: Yes.

She: What is your great idea?

He: My great idea is that we become a team.

She: What a great idea!

He: I thought that you would like my great idea.

She: Yes, they were a bit repetitious but perhaps it would work.

Both: It just might work!

She: But they had a perplexing challenge.

He: What kind of sport will we play?

She: I don't know. But with your speed and my grace, certainly we'll succeed at whatever we try.

He: Basketball?

Jennifer: I'm too short. Gymnastics?

He: I'm too stocky. Shot put?

She: I'm too weak. Skiing?

He: Too cold. Canoeing?

She: Too hot. Synchronized swimming?

He: I can't swim. Marathons?

She: Weak shins. Potato? *(pronounced as in familiar song)*

He: Potato.

She: Tomato?

He: Tomato.

Both: Let's call the whole thing off!

He: But they didn't. Their love for athletics and the drive to be the best they could be, along with a little mutual admiration, gave birth to a totally new sport.

She: The leaping, pirouetting,

He: twenty- meter dash

She: to Beethoven's Ode to Joy found in his 9th symphony.

He: On your mark, get set, go!

*The music begins. **Jerry** makes speed his primary goal while taking a few small jumps. **Jennifer**, on the other hand, spins and leaps gracefully and slowly to the finish line. Before she gets to the finish line Jerry interrupts—*

He: All right! Cut the music!

She: Wait! I wasn't finished!

He: This isn't working out. I thought we were supposed to be a team!

She: How am I supposed to be a member of a duet if my partner keeps leaving me in the dust? Besides, I thought you were supposed to catch me when I did the backwards leap.

He: If I stuck around to catch you, I'd be adding three and a half seconds to my time.

She: You and your silly stopwatch! Can't you put that thing down for one rehearsal?

He: I don't see how your can do this with that music droning in the background. I'm falling asleep before we get to the finish line.

She: My dance teacher told me that to experience life to the fullest, we must not rush.

He: My coach said play hard or go home to mama!

She: You're not helping me!

He: And you think that you're helping me?

Both: Why can't we do it *my* way?

She: *(to audience)* As you can see, Jerry and Jennifer are at a standstill. *(Jerry is still frozen)* No pun intended. They are frozen by unmet needs in the relationship.

Jerry starts doing workout routines.

She: Jerry believed that Jennifer should lift weights and do more aerobics. He wanted Jennifer to be like he was. But he understood that his intimidating style of leadership only served to aggravate the situation. He was disappointed.

He slouches in frustration.

He: I'm disappointed.

She: But as he pouted, he encountered a wonderful moment of inspiration!

He: Look! A wonderful moment of inspiration! Why don't I try to learn what she likes so well. Secretly, of course. It's not a very macho compromise.

She: So Jerry went to the Acme School of Dance.

Jerry begins practicing ballet moves.

She: And believe it or not, he liked it! He didn't like it as much as the 100-meter dash but he developed a greater appreciation for Jennifer and broadened his horizons.

He: I feel broadened! *(as Narrator)* Jennifer was very impressed.

She: I'm impressed!

He: So impressed was Jennifer that she decided to improve her versatility. *(Jennifer mimes the actions.)* She did what most people do when they want to improve themselves She went shopping!

She: Do you have any shoes with the cute little pump on them? On sale?!

He: After buying three or four pairs she began an incredible schedule of aerobics, stair stepping, bench pressing, side-straddle hopping, and fork lifting

She: Fork lifting??

He: You know. Eating the right kind of foods. Fork lifting—get it? Never mind.

She: Jerry couldn't believe what he was seeing. Jennifer had improved her speed and agility in less than two weeks.

He: It's gotta be the shoes!

Both: And they both grew as individuals and as a team.

She: Perhaps these experiences will help them resolve even more important issues in their relationship such as housework. . .

He: fishing trips,

She: poetry,

He: football,

She: bad breath,

He: wall paper designs,

She: athletic socks turned inside-out in the laundry bin;

He: as well as

She: wonderful weekends,

He: moonlit walks,

She: bubble baths,

He: secret weekend rendezvous,

She: long passionate kisses,

He: unbridled laughter,

She: coupled with moments of shared dreams,

He: tears of sorrow and joy,

She: intimate conversations by candlelight ,

He: secrets held between two of one flesh

She: as wives,

He: as husbands,

Both: as friends and lovers.

LOOKS

Glances, stares, and glares...

She: At first there was the glance.

He: I saw her in a crowded room,

She: through the noise and the obstacles

He: I saw her.

She: I was suspended in time,

He: weightless—

She: —it was back when we both were skinny—

He: —motionless.

She: He said he was frozen by my beauty.

He: Or maybe the air conditioning was up too high.

She: There I was.

He: And there I was.

Both: We were *both* there,

He: together,

She: and yet we knew not each other.

He: We were void of name and telephone number.

She: We were strangers.

He: I glanced.

She: And I glanced.

Both: Oh what glances!

She: At first, short glances, but very soon the glances turned into stares.

He: We stared at each other and we liked what we saw.

She: We stared over dinner

He: at fancy restaurants;

She: we stared at each other during church

He: when we should have been staring at the pastor.

She: He would even stare during football games.

He: She would even stare during clearance sales.

She: We ogled.

He: Funny word but quite fitting.

She: Ogle—Webster defines it as—"to stare with great desire."

He: We were in love!

She: And our glances turned into stares.

He: Then we wanted to see more of each other.

She: We desired each other.

He: We wanted to stare at each other all the time,

She: day and night,

He: in sickness and in health,

She: till death do us part.

He: So we stared at the altar.

She: And we received a license to stare.

He: Then

She: very shortly after we received permission to stare

He: day and night,

She: night and day,

He: all the time.

Both: We saw *everything*.

She: And the stares turned into glares.

He: Sorry I'm late! We played an extra nine holes.

She: Glare.

He: Happy Birthday, Honey. You'll love this new drill!

She: Glare.

He: How about tonight?

She: I'm too tired...

He: Glare.

She: Then—

He: football.

She: Glare.

He: More football.

She: Glare.

He: No more football.

She: Great!

He: But more basketball.

She: Glare.

He: Then—

She: waiting while I roll my hair.

He: Glare.

She: Another pair of shoes.

He: Glare.

She: Long distance phone calls.

He: Glare.

She: And so the story goes.

He: And the more we glared the less we stared.

She: We never again thought about ogling, but a stare every now and then would be nice.

He: We can raise kids, climb the ladder, go to church.

She: We can do just about anything without looking at each other.

He: Don't we want to see?

She: I'm his wife. He once glanced my way and said "Wow!"

He: I'm her husband. She used to love to look at me; and now it seems that the only time she looks is when she wants something.

She: Not only does he not look at me, he doesn't even look at what I do! He thinks that clean socks just fly from the hamper into the washer then to the dryer and then back to the drawer.

He: She looked at me with such respect! Now she doesn't even care about my needs.

She: Making love—what a misnomer! It's turned into a duty. How can I enjoy intimacy with someone who doesn't even look at me? Deeply.

He: Before I was married, I used to laugh at the way the King James Version describes sex as "knowing." Now I understand. How can you make love with someone who doesn't even know you—much less someone who doesn't look at you?

She: Is there a cure for blindness?

He: Is there surgery that can remove emotional cataracts?

She: It all started with a glance.

He: Can we find that glance?

She: Will we look at each other?

He: Deeply?

Both: Will we?

He: If anyone is in Christ

She: he is a new

He: she is a new

Both: creation.

He: God has reconciled us to Himself through the incredible gift of Jesus Christ.

She: And now God has given us a new ministry.

He: The ministry of reconciliation.

She: That look—the fire of the relationship lost because of circumstance,

He: hurt,

She: fear,

He: anger,

She: and misunderstandings.

Both: That look can be found through Christ.

THE INSPECTORS

A marital pop-quiz

He: I beg of you

She: present your bodies

He: as a living sacrifice

She: holy

He: and acceptable unto God

She: which is an act of worship.

He: Don't conform to the ways of this world,

Both: but be transformed

She: by the renewing of your mind.

He: Do you not know that your body is the temple of the Holy Spirit

She: who is in you?

He: And you are not your own.

Beat.

She: Knock, knock.

He: *(opening the door)* Yes. Can I help you?

She: Is this the body, heart, mind, and soul of John Smith?

He: Why yes, it is. What do you—

She: I'm the inspector.

He: Inspector?

She: Right.

He: I wasn't expecting an inspector—

She: If you knew that an inspector was coming, it wouldn't be much of an inspection would it?

He: I guess not. What do you need to inspect?

She: Several things, If you'll excuse me. *(She walks right in.)* Let me see that thought life. *(looking in at a focal point as if it were a meter)* Hmm. Not good. Several patterns seem to be developing here. Something's wrong and yet we'll never quite understand it completely until we look over here at the eyes. *(inspecting)* Just as I thought.

He: What?

She: Wandering eyes.

He: Wandering eyes?

She: Your eyes seem to be having trouble. You've lost control over them. They get fixated. Like at the grocery store counter where you can't keep your eyes off that "Cosmo." And that "Sports Illustrated" that you had to buy. You told your wife that there was an article on the decline of bowling in the past decade. You know good and well that you bought it because it was the February "swimsuit issue."

He: I am a big bowling fan.

She: Get real, Pinocchio. Don't you see that the thought control center is being corroded by the wandering eye?

He: What's wrong with a few peeks?

She: What's wrong with a few peeks?? Were you born yesterday? Let's come over here to the comparison valve.

He: The comparison valve?

She: Look. It's totally overflowing. You see, every time the wandering eyes short circuit the thought life, the comparison valve overflows. You become so preoccupied with these images, that your comparison valve works over time. You compare your wife—who by the way is an incredible woman—with Julia Roberts, Cindy Crawford, Dolly Parton—

He: Dolly Parton??

She: —Cybil Shepherd, and on and on until the comparison valve overruns the reality monitor.

He: Sounds scary.

She: *(She back hands him in the stomach.)* Stick that chest out and look me in the eye when I'm talking to you, John. This is not good. Not good at all. Let's take a look at the intimacy measuring system.

He: The intimacy measuring system? What's that all about?

She: It monitors your intimacy output. Toward your wife of course. *(looks at an imaginary meter)* Ouch! You've got some real problems here. In the past week you held your wife's hand only twice, you gave her only one full body hug and three side shoulder hugs. You deposited two "I love yous" and three "Love yas." You did have some romantic moments with her, but the foreplay time was incredibly short.

He: Foreplay ... What's that?

She: That's exactly what I mean. And by the way, the teeth maintenance log says that on Saturdays you usually don't brush your teeth until around 11 am.

He: You don't miss anything, do you?

She: Not much, John. If things don't get better soon, I'm going to have to take away your license.

He: My marriage license?

She: No. Not your marriage license. Your manhood license!

He: *(as Narrator now)* This inspection program could work two ways.

She: It could?

He: It could. Knock, knock!

She: Who is it?

He: You know who it is! Now open up.

She: Not the inspector!

He: Yes, the inspector!

She: What do you want to see?

He: Let's start with a look at the thought life. *(looks at the meter)* Not bad but I'm getting some frequent Kevin Costner and Tom Cruise entries. Don't you know that the comparison valve will cause a melt down?! Besides, all those action scenes are done by stunt men. And what's this? "The Young and the Restless"? Bad news! And the excitement output valve is at a dangerously low ebb!

She: It is?

He: You've worn that night gown that goes all the way down to your ankles for the past month. It has 32 buttons on it. What happened to that satin negligee that you got at your "for girls only" wedding shower?

She: I think I cut it up to use for a VBS craft.

He: Very valiant excuse, but don't you know that sex is a ministry, too!

She: It is?

He: Of course it is! Not once every three months like a Sunday School quarterly. By the way, let's take a look at the surprise monitor. It's too dusty to even read! When's the last time you've laid a passionate kiss on him in the middle of the day?

She: Well, there was the—

He: When's the last time he crawled into bed without noticing the wildly passionate woman waiting for his routine hug so that she could seize him in wild ruthless passion.

She: If some woman ever did that to him I would—

He: I'm not talking about another woman! I'm talking about you! You, Edwina! It's surprise! It's intrigue! Not this "wake me up when it's over" business! Not this "I just changed the sheets, so we better not mess 'em up" attitude. Not this "one of the kids might skip school and see us making a splash in the bathtub" frame of mind.

She: You're serious, aren't you.

He: Of course I am. I wouldn't suggest that you do it all in one day. But think of it this way, there are more places to start a fire than the fire place. Try the kitchen, the couch, the garage—

She: The garage?

He: *(thoughtfully)* Okay. Maybe not the garage, but when in doubt, try the bedroom. I'll be back in two weeks. Buy some fire insurance, and have fun.

Both: But thanks be to the grace of God!

He: Inspectors don't burst into lives with condemnation and ridicule.

She: Still, there is a loving voice calling out to us—

He: wanting the best for us—

She: so that we will want the best for each other.

He: We may be rough, unkempt, and lazy—

She: We might drive our husbands and children crazy—

He: We might not pass inspection or test.

She: Still, a voice calls us to be our best.

He: A pure, holy, and living sacrifice.

She: To remember our salvation, the incredible price.

He: Just as Christ loves the Church, so we should love our wives

She: and give our husbands the best of our lives

Both: as a holy and living sacrifice!

Scripts For Worship

AND THE ROCKS CRY OUT
by Jim Tippens

This creative vignette could be done with or without costuming (or should we say rockstuming!). Kids and adults will enjoy the humor and imagination found in this short piece.

Adapted from: *Luke 19:40*

Cast: *Rocky, Bo, Jesus, Narrator; also good for Puppets.*

Scene: *Two rocks are quietly sitting out in a field, doing, whatever rocks do!*

Rocky: Hey! Bo! Or do you still prefer being called Mr. Boulder?

Bo: Yo, Rocky! My name is my life! I know it's a hard thing to grasp. But it is!

Rocky: Did you hear the racket those kids were making the other day? I thought they were going to pick me up and throw me!

Bo: That was really cool. You know, I thought of a great name for the music those teenagers listen to! "Us and Roll Music." What do you think?

Rocky: It might catch on in a couple thousand years from now. But we've got plenty of time!

Bo: You got that right.

Rocky: Hey, who's that guy walking this way?

Bo: I don't know. But I hope He doesn't get tired and sit on me! Those long Jewish robes smother me.

Rocky: He's got some others with him but they're staying back there in the grove. *(excitedly)* Hey! He's coming our way!

Bo: Be still; maybe he won't notice us. I get so tired of people taking us away and building things out of us! A temple here—a wall there—an altar there—

Rocky: Shhh!

Jesus comes into view and kneels next to the rocks.

Rocks: Bo. What's He doing?

Bo: He'll probably pull out a chisel and start sculpting or something.

Rocky: I don't want to end up like old Stoney!

Bo: What happened to him?

Rocky: They wrote a song about him. *(singing)* "Rock of Ages, cleft for me."

Bo: It looks like He's praying.

Rocky: Must be like the Babylonians—they used to worship us!

Bo: I don't think He's praying to us. He's only praying near us.

Rocky: You've got that right! What's that? Is it raining?

Bo: No. It's—I think those are tears! I see His lips moving. Can you hear what He's saying?

Rocky: I think He said, "Not My will but Yours be done."

Bo: He looks determined now. He's going back to the others.

Jesus walks away.

Rocky: Not what I was expecting.

Bo: What do you think that was all about?

Rocky: I don't know.

Bo: It seemed sort of sad and yet peaceful. You don't think He's—

Rocky: Could be—

Bo: It must be! I feel like something has—

Rocky: I feel it too!

Bo: Something has come over me! I can't help myself!

Rocky: Me neither!

Bo: What are we doing? *Praise God!*

Rocky: I don't know—*Hallelujah!*

Bo: What did you call me?? *Glory!*

Rocky: It must have been Jesus!

Both: *Praise the Lord! Hallelujah!*

Rocky: That's Him! The One who created us!

Both: *Praise the King! Jesus Christ!*

Scripture Reader: And Jesus told the Pharisees that if His disciples were told to stop speaking about Him, the stones along the road would burst into cheers.

~

HOLY SPIRIT
by Matt Tullos

Cast: *Scripture Reader, Man 1, Man 2, Woman 1, Woman 2, Woman 3*

Man 1: Lord, we come to you as broken instruments. We are unworthy to share in Your grace. How can we teach of such a holy God to a world that sees our flaws, our scars, our failures? How can we minister?

Scripture Reader: You have been made competent ministers of a new covenant, not of the letter but of the Spirit. For the letter kills but the Spirit gives new life. *(2 Cor. 3:6, paraphrase)*

Woman 1: As a mother, how can I know Your will? I struggle between knowing Your will and my desire. My faith seems worthless.

Scripture Reader: The Spirit will help you in your weakness. You do not know what to pray for, but the Holy Spirit Himself will intercede for you with groans that words cannot express. *(Romans 8:26, paraphrase)*

Man 2: It seems like I'm in a constant tug-of-war. Like Paul, I struggle daily to remain faithful.

Scripture Reader: The flesh sets its desire against the Spirit and the Spirit against the flesh, for these are in opposition to one another. But if you are led by the Spirit, you are free.

Woman 2: Lord, I desire to serve You. But in the heat of the battle, I'm so easily given to retreat. I lack the power to be victorious.

Scripture Reader: You shall receive power when the Holy Spirit comes upon you, and you shall be My witnesses. *(Acts 1:8, paraphrase)*

Man 1: Lord, You've called us to minister. How? What shall I do? Where should I go?

Scripture Reader: The Holy Spirit, whom the Father will send, will teach you all things and will remind you of everything I have said to you. *(John 14:26, paraphrase)*

Woman 3: Father, teach us to worship. Help us to seek You in all things.

Scripture Reader: "God is Spirit, and they that worship Him must worship in spirit and truth." *(John 4:24, NASB)*

Man 2: Lord, we are here to worship You.

Woman 2: To lift Your name above all names...

Man 1 and Woman 3: Holy Spirit, teach us. Minister to us as we worship and adore our God.

All: In the name of the Father, the Son, and the Holy Spirit.

HEALED AT THE GATE
by Anna Belle Nihart

A lame man wanting a handout received a miracle!

*Could also be used with **Puppets**.*

Watch this! *(Man jumps up and down, turns around).*

Not very remarkable? It is to me. You see, only a few days ago I was lame. I'd never walked, a birth defect. You're asking, "How did he provide for his needs?" Well, I couldn't farm or tend a flock. That's obvious. I couldn't make any goods to sell in the market for I had no materials. I supported myself by begging.

My location was at the temple. I was carried daily and left at the gate everyone called "Beautiful." As good Jews entered the temple for prayer, sacrifices, or lively debates, I would ask for coins. They were usually pretty obliging, especially if they were in a crowd. I learned my trade pretty well!

One afternoon around three o'clock, I saw a confident pair of men coming my way. "Alms!" I cried out. They stopped. That's always a good sign. One of the men, Peter, said he had no silver or gold. I thought to myself: "Then move on." Tip: no one will stop if others are standing around you. They just move by quickly without any eye contact.

The man, Peter, continued, "I will give you what I have." I wasn't disappointed. Perhaps he will offer me food or something I can trade later. Then, unbelievably, he ordered me to stand up. While I was thinking of this cruel command, he took my hands and lifted me. I stood! I stood alone!

Peter and his friend, John, had performed a miracle. They said it was in the name of Jesus. That name rang through me. Everyone around the temple had heard of the teacher from Nazareth who had been crucified and walked out of His tomb three days later. The news of Jesus' resurrection had really caused a big stir around here!

Oh, back to my story. I began jumping and hopping and laughing and crying all at once. It was the greatest moment of my life. I could walk. I was healed. The three of us entered the temple. You should have seen the look on everyone's face when they recognized me as the beggar from the Beautiful Gate. *(laughing)* It was priceless.

Peter seized the moment to tell the good men about his power. He told them it came from Jesus. He went on to deliver a most powerful sermon. Some people said I was just healed in order to provide Peter a vehicle to deliver his message about Jesus. Others said I was simply in the right place at the right time. Maybe so. All I know is that all my life I had been a receiver. Now I am a giver. I have a miraculous story to tell everyone I meet. I can tell them about a *different* gate that is beautiful; a gate that heals the soul. I can tell them how to enter into eternal life through Jesus Christ. That's the real miracle.

THY WILL BE DONE
by Rod Payne

Or how not to pray in several lessons

Adapted from: *Matthew 6: 9-13, KJV*

*This work is in the form of a readers theatre with the addition of a **Character** who plays off the chorus. The individual **Reader's** lines may be assigned to the number of persons participating—with the option of having only one person serve in this capacity.*

Reader: One day Jesus was praying in a certain place.

Character: Ever wonder where that certain place was?

Reader: Ahem! When He finished, one of His disciples said to Him—

Character: Lord, teach us to pray, just like John taught his disciples.

Reader: He said to them, "When you pray, say: Our Father, which art in Heaven, hallowed be thy name, Thy kingdom come. . ."

Character: That's the first part I wanted to talk to you about, the kingdom stuff. I know it's supposed to come but I'd like to have all of mine now, if I could. I like the idea of kind of having my own personal ministry right here, you know, my kingdom where people thank me for all the good I've done for them. It never hurts to have people grateful to you. I think I'll pray for more opportunities for public, and I do mean public, service.

Reader: Everyone who exalts himself will be humbled and he who humbles himself will be exalted.

Character: I was just asking for a little help in that direction, that's all.

Reader: "Thy will be done in Earth as it is in Heaven."

Character: But that's just the point, His will isn't done here on Earth. Everyday millions go to their grave without knowing Christ as their Savior. How do I pray for them?

Reader: Ask the Lord of the harvest to send out workers into His harvest fields. You go and proclaim the kingdom of God.

Character: Hey, that's a little personal, isn't it? When things get personal in my prayers I like to be on the receiving end, you know like getting stuff, not being told where to go or what to do.

Reader: "Give us this day our daily bread."

Character: That's more like it. It never hurts to have more than enough.

Reader: Man does not live by bread alone.

Character: Then why ask for things at all?

Reader: You will have plenty to eat until you are full *and* you will praise the name of the Lord your God.

Character: I guess He likes us to know where our blessings are from.

100

Reader: Every good and perfect gift is from above. Ahem!

Character: What? You mean there's more? I kinda thought this prayer business could end with me asking for stuff and God giving it to me.

Reader: "Forgive us our trespasses"

Character: Wait a minute. Wait just a minute. I didn't say I had done anything wrong.

Reader: "For all have sinned and come short of the Glory of God."

Character: Oh, that. Well yeah, maybe I've done some things to some people but believe me they had it coming. It was them against me and they started it.

Reader: "As we forgive those who have trespassed against us."

Character: Oh, no. I don't mind asking God for things. I don't even mind thanking Him for them, but I sure don't want Him to forgive me the same way I forgive others. Man, I'd never make it into Heaven.

Reader: "And lead us not into temptation but deliver us from evil."

Character: Sure, I wouldn't expect God to lead me into sin, but I don't know that I need to ask Him to keep me away from a little temptation now and then. I know how to control things; I can keep a little sin under control now and then.

Reader: The sinful mind is hostile to God.

Character: Hostile? You don't mean like at odds with. If you're fighting with somebody they're probably not going to want to give you anything or keep you from anything or . . .

Reader: Count yourselves dead to sin. Those controlled by the sinful nature cannot please God.

Character: Oh.

Reader: Ahem! "For thine is the kingdom and the power and the glory for ever."

Character: This isn't turning out like I thought it would. I thought I had this praying part figured out. I thought it was kind of like I do all this asking and then God comes through with all this giving. The way it sounds it's like it's all directed toward Him. *His* is the *kingdom*, the *power,* and the *glory.*

Reader: "To Him who is able to keep you from falling and to present you before His glorious presence without fault and with great joy,"

Reader(s): To the only God *our Savior*, be glory, majesty, power, and authority through Jesus Christ our Lord.

Character: It really is His kingdom, isn't it? The whole ball of wax; it's all His. He's the only reason any of us exists at all. It's not supposed to be a wishing well; it has to be a time of recognizing God for who He is. But to really get to know somebody, you've got to spend time with him.

AN OPENING PRAYER
by Matt Tullos

Use this call to worship with several readers

Cast: *Readers 1, 2, 3*

1: Father, just being in Your presence changes us.

2: We want to abide in You.

3: We want the word of Christ to dwell in us richly.

1: We worship You through songs, hymns, and spiritual songs, singing with grace in our hearts to you.

2: You, oh Lord are our only hope.

3: We know you as the sower who plants the seed of truth in our lives.

1: We know you as the one who saw us on the road.

2: You didn't pass us by as others did. You stopped and healed our wounds. You did not look at our outward appearance.

3: When we were all alone You saw our hearts and our needs.

1: You loved us still.

2: How can we express our gratefulness to You, Father.

3: This is love—not that we love you, but that You love us.

1: You gave us your only Son. We don't know why. Your love and grace can't be explained.

2: Despite our failure,

3: Despite our scars,

1: Despite our fear,

2: Despite shortcomings that are too many to count,

3: You loved us without condition, reason, or gain.

1: Your Son, Your only Son was broken and pierced for us.

2: How could we ever say *no* to You.

3: Accept our praise as a humble acknowledgement of Your steadfast love.

~

COME TO US
by Thomas H. Cairns

Dramatic introduction to "Come, Thou Long-Expected Jesus"

Cast: *Narrator, #1, #2, #3, #4*

#1 stands lifting hands and eyes heavenward, as if pleading to God.

Narrator: Come to us, Lord Jesus, Prince of Peace, because we are wracked with war in Bosnia, Cambodia, Columbia, and on the streets of our cities.

#1 sits as #2 stands immediately in the same posture.

Narrator: Come to us, Lord Jesus, baby born in a cattle stall, because we're killing our babies in the womb, and many of the ones who are born are beaten, starved, unloved, undisciplined, and forgotten.

#2 sits as #3 stands immediately in the same posture.

Narrator: Come to us, Lord Jesus, feeder of multitudes, because we are unemployed, underpaid, burdened with national debt, beset by the greedy who legally and illegally steal and waste our hard-earned wealth and business capital.

#3 sits as #4 stands immediately in the same posture.

Narrator: Come to us, Lord Jesus, Savior of prostitutes, filthy lepers, and the comfortably religious people; we are our own worst enemies. We are sinful and flawed; we aren't wise enough or powerful enough to solve the world's problems or our own—but You can heal us; You can forgive us; You can make us new on the inside. Come, thou long-expected Jesus, come in this hour of worship.

#1, #2, #3, stand with #4 and motion for the congregation to stand as the song leader announces the hymn, "Come, Thou Long-Expected Jesus," and asks people to stand and sing. (The Baptist Hymnal, 1991, No. 77)

SHOUT!
by Matt Tullos

Adapted from: *Psalm 100, Matthew 28; Mark 8, 10; Luke 3; and John 1, 4, 10*

Leader: Shout for joy to the Lord all the earth.

Choir: John shouted, "Prepare the way of the Lord."

Congregation: Worship the Lord with gladness.

Choir: Jesus replied, "God is spirit, and His worshippers must worship in spirit and truth."

Congregation: Come before Him with joyful songs.

Choir: The crowd sang, "Hosanna: Blessed is He who comes in the name of the Lord."

Congregation: Know that the Lord is God.

Choir: John testified, "In the beginning was the Word, and the Word was with God, and the Word was God."

Congregation: It is He who made us and we are His.

Choir: "Through Him all things were made, without Him nothing was made that had been made."

Congregation: We are His people and the sheep of His pasture.

Choir: Jesus said, "I am the good Shepherd. The good Shepherd lays down His life for the sheep."

Congregation: Enter His gates with thanksgiving.

Choir: Therefore Jesus said again, "I tell you the truth, I am the gate for the sheep."

Congregation: Give thanks to Him and praise His name.

Choir: Peter replied, "You are the Christ, the Son of the living God."

Congregation: For the Lord is good and His love endures forever.

Choir: Jesus promised, "Surely I am with you always, to the very end of the age."

Congregation: His faithfulness continues through all generations.

All: And all God's people said, "Hallelujah!" and "Amen!"

Praise God For His Great Love

by Charles Dorris

Try using these with choruses of praise

Cast: *Sixteen Readers*

Life!

1: "These are written that ye might believe that Jesus is the Christ, the Son of God, and that believing, ye might have life through his name." *(John 20:31, KJV)*

1,2,3: *Life* through his name

1,2,3,4,5: *Life . . . through His Name*

All: *Life . . . through His Name*

6: Overflowing life

7: Abundant life

8: Eternal life

6: Jesus came to us, calling his sheep by name

7: Calling in the voice of a loving shepherd

8: Calling in the voice of a loving father

6: Jesus comes to us, calling out across the walls of our sickness, our sadness, our sin.

7: Come unto me.

8: You are mine.

6: I have called you *by name.*

Here Is Love!

9: Herein is love, not that we loved God, but that He loved us, and sent his son to (die for) our sins. *(1 John 4:10, paraphrase)*

All: Here's love!

10: Love . . . reaching down to me

11: Down to the bottom of the pit where my sins had imprisoned me

9: Love entering the realm of the hopeless

10: Love lifting me up to Him

11: Love taking away my sin and guilt

9,10,11: "When the fullness of the time was come, God sent forth His Son." *(Gal. 4:4, KJV)*

4: God sent His Son.

3: He came unto His own, and His own received Him not.

1: Imposter!

2: Madman!

3: Heretic!

4: Devil!

5: "But as many as received him, to them gave he power to become the sons of God, even to those who believe on his name." *(John 1:12, KJV)*

10: That's love!

11: That's love!

12: That's love!

6: That's grace!

7: God's loving Grace!

All: *For me!!!*

Nothing Can Separate Us

7: In love Jesus died, believing that God would raise Him up.

7,8: He did.

9: He is the one who died for us.

10: And came back to life again for us.

11: And is sitting at the place of highest honor next to God, pleading for us there in Heaven.

12: Overwhelming victory is ours through Christ who loved us enough to die for us.

1: We are convinced

2,3: We are convinced

1,2,3: We are convinced

1,2,3: That *nothing*

4,5,6,7: *(builds) Nothing*

8,9,10,11,12: *(builds more) Nothing*

1: Can ever separate us from His love.

2: Death can't.

3: And life can't.

4: The angels won't.

5: And all the powers of hell itself cannot keep God's love away! *(Romans 8, selected verses)*

6: Do *you* live in that love?

13: Have you acknowledged to yourself that you are a sinner?

14: Have you admitted it to others?

15: Have you confessed it to God?

16: Have you opened your heart to the truth of God's love?

13: Will you invite him into your life? (beat) This is what you do . . .

This Is the Way To Life!

10: Lord Jesus, I confess that I am a sinner, Lost and confused and dying. I call upon you to forgive my sins, To give me a place in your family, and to live in me from this time and forever.

Even Numbers: Lord, we are *all* sinners, saved by your grace.

Odd Numbers: "Take away our bent to sinning. Alpha and Omega be; End of faith as its beginning, Set our hearts at liberty." *(Stanza two from "Love Divine, All Loves Excelling," The Baptist Hymnal, 1991, No. 208)*

1: "You shall know the truth, and the truth shall make you free. And if the Son shall make you free, you shall be free indeed" *(John 8:32,36, KJV)*

Free Indeed!

2: Freedom is. . . space. Room to run and leap and play.

3: Room to move freely without bumping into people.

4: Room to grow

5: Freedom is . . . time. Not always having to rush and push

6: Time to sit and think. Time to take a quiet walk, or go fishing

7: Time to read or play the piano
Or to do what you like best

8: Freedom is the right to choose

9: To choose my friends

10: To choose my vocation

11: To choose—*(interruption)*

12: Hey, wait! How can a person be free if he's a slave to Christ?

11: What?

12: How are you free if God is holding all the trump cards?

11: I can't explain it. I can just *feel* it and *know* it. Our faith is often expressed in opposites— strength in weakness—greatness in service—life in death— freedom in submission

13: May our attitude be the same as that of Christ Jesus, ". . .who being in the form of God thought it not robbery to be equal with God, But made himself of no reputation, and took upon him the form of a servant, and was made in the likeness of men: and being found in fashion as a man, He humbled himself, and became obedient unto death, Even the death of the cross.

14: "Wherefore God also hath highly exalted him, and given him a name which is above every name, That at the name of—

All: "*Jesus*

14: "—every knee should bow, Of things in heaven, and things in earth, and things under the earth; and that every tongue should confess that—

All: "Jesus Christ is Lord

15,16: "To the glory of God the Father."
(Phil. 2:5-11, KJV)

All: Jesus is Lord!

All: *(building)* Jesus is Lord!

All: *(with great enthusiasm)* Jesus is Lord!!!

YOU HEARD MY CRY
by Matt Tullos

Creatively divide this reading for several readers. The congregation could be asked to participate by saying the phrase "You heard my cry"

Father, I praise you.

You heard my cry.

When anger and loneliness loitered in the halls of my soul,

You heard my cry.

When the future seemed too far away to bring comfort,

You heard my cry.

When the aching moments of yesterday slipped in through the back door,

You heard my cry.

When irritation and confusion danced on the roof top so much that the shingles were dislodged and the rains of despair brought forth the mildew of discontentment,

You heard my cry.

When there was nowhere to turn,

You heard my cry.

When my soul ached for companionship and affection,

You heard my cry.

When I was paralyzed by nightmares and I wept at midday for fear of the night,

You heard my cry.

When my hand reaches out to yours and I feel the nail-pierced scar, I give thanks because before I was ever born,

You heard my cry.

Hallelujah!

PILATE
by Rick Shoemaker

A simple yet effective monologue for Easter worship or Bible study

Pilate, washing hands in frustration.

Who was this Man? Who was this Jesus?

Others I have crucified. Why does this Man's death torment me?

He is but another Jew! the world is far better with one less of them! Even the King of the Jews.

A king without subjects! Why did His followers remain silent? Why was their voice not heard? "Barabbas or Jesus?" I said! "It is your decision! I will release one of them as is the custom during this Passover season! It is your decision."

I am not to blame for the death of this Man! King of the Jews, if the voice of Your people had spoken, I would have set You free! You died because of Your own people, not because of me. *(Washes his hands again.)*

He was from Galilee. Herod, He was your responsibility—not mine! You have accused me of infringing on your jurisdiction. You have complained to Rome of this! So I left the judgement to you. He was a Galilean! You could have freed Him! Why did you return Him to me? *(Washes hands again.)*

I had no choice. No choice! I could not release Him. These Jews are a stubborn people. If I had let Him go they would have complained to Caesar. They would have accused me of treason.

I would have lost my place of authority in the Empire.

Jesus, I gave You the chance to deny You were a king. "My kingdom is not of this world." What does that mean? You could have been free if You had denied You were the Son of God! Son of God! Son of God! Of which God? Of Jupiter? Of Mars? Of Neptune? Yes, the son of Neptune—god of the sea! They say You walk upon the water!

Or perhaps the Son of the God of the Jews! A weak God indeed!

If You are the Son of God, then Your Father has forsaken You! How could a God let His Son be crucified? Then your Father is to blame; not me!

Continues washing hands.

Business as Usual
by Rod Payne

Cast: *Four Voices*

Voice 1: David's son Solomon was granted the task of building the temple for the Lord of Israel. He was awarded the contract for the place which would symbolize God's presence among His people. When the work was completed, Solomon gathered the chief priests and elders of the children of Israel together—

Voice 2: —to dedicate the temple. And to worship the one, true God.

Voice 1: "And it came to pass, when the priests were come out of the holy place, that The Cloud filled the House of the Lord.

Voice 3: The Cloud?

Voice 4: Yes, the physical representation of God.

Voice 1: "So that the priests could not minister because of the cloud: for the glory of the Lord had filled the house of the Lord."

Voice 3: Wait a minute.

Voice 4: The priests couldn't minister because they were scared of that cloud!

Voice 1: No, because God was there in a mighty way.

Voice 3: Oh . . . .

Voice 2: They couldn't *(pause)* minister?

Voice 4: They couldn't work. They couldn't do their jobs.

Voice 3: Hey, you mean . . .

Voice 4: Right, they couldn't, uh, they couldn't follow the *printed order of service?*

Voice 2: You don't mean it. Why that's etched in stone, or at least printed in stone in the bulletin.

Voice 3: How did they know what to do next?

Voice 1: They couldn't conduct business as usual.

Voice 2: No special music just before the sermon?

Voice 3: No lengthy announcements right after the first two songs and right before the welcome of the guests?

Voice 2: No three points and a poem or sometimes a joke?

Voices 2&3: *No offering*!?!?!?!

Voice 2: No counting the number of verses sung in the invitation and wondering if t+he service will go past noon?

Voice 3: What *did* they have if they didn't have the framework of years of tradition to keep their service together?

Voice 1: The presence of the living God. The God of Abraham, Isaac, and Jacob. The One Who is Who He is!

Voice 3: Oh . . .

Voice 2: If we have a choice . . .

Voice(s): Yes?

Voice 2: I'd like to try it some Sunday with the Cloud.

MARY
by Jean W. Beasley

Christmas Portraits

He's a good baby—I think that and I have to laugh! Good? He's God's own son! Anyway, He really is a good boy. He's not fussy, and when He does cry, it's usually in a way I can take, because I can do something about it, though I'm not always sure what! It's usually something easy—hunger, a mess to clean up, a hurt to soothe—and then I get to kiss it and make it better. And He often laughs! But sometimes He has such a sorrowful, lonely cry. What does He long for? What does He need? The other day—oh! How can a cry like that come from such a tiny baby? And I'm useless then; I can't make it better!

Joseph doesn't like for me to dwell on all this--he's a fine husband, very practical, and he also doesn't like to see me sad. Besides, he's right in that Jesus doesn't seem the worse for it; and Jesus was so sweet the last time—I hadn't even realized that I was crying, too. I just wanted to hug Him 'til He was happy again. But, do you know, when He calmed down after being like that, He seemed to be trying to comfort me? The old man . . . Simeon, was it? Yes . . . when we took Jesus to the temple, Simeon said that my heart would be pierced. I think, when my son cries at those times, I think he was right.

But, when Jesus calls me, and I put aside whatever's occupying my time right then and just go to Him—those are the times that I know that all of this is worth it.

JOSEPH
by Jean W. Beasley
Christmas Portraits

This is—too much. This is exactly what I wanted and expected from life—what I've always prayed for: a godly wife and a fine, healthy son. But, oh, my God—my God! What have You done to me? I don't think I can handle this!

I was afraid to hold Him, at first. Just how do you handle the son of God, literally or figuratively? God, how can I be a father to Jesus, knowing that You are His father? Mary says that, when you get right down to it, You are every baby's father, ultimately, and she wishes that more earthly fathers realized it. I agree that a lot of evil in this world could be avoided if fathers took their responsibility to You more seriously, God. But I wouldn't wish this on anyone. The son of God . . .!

I fell in love with His little wrinkly face, though . . . and all that hair! He's lost a lot of it. Of course, I love to hold Him now. I feel at my best, somehow, when I am close to Him. When I'm just thinking about Him, and my relationship to Him, I can get confused and overwhelmed by all this, believe me. But, when I am actually with Him, talking with Him and falling in love with Him all over again, well, I'm still confused, often enough, but I have great hope, despite the pressures I'm under. And Mary's right, He does love me. I can tell.

ANNA
by Jean W. Beasley

Christmas Portraits

I love this place, this temple. I've practically lived here for years! *(beat)* Some of you younger ones seem startled to hear me talk—I've become quite a fixture, haven't I? The walls might as well have spoken, you seem so taken aback. Your parents have heard me, though, a time or two—and some even listened. What? You thought "prophetess" was some kind of nickname? Ha!

The house of the Lord—I know this place very well, and I have tried to know my God. I know that the scale of these rooms, amazing as they are—100 cubits high, did you know that?—does not really do the scale of God any justice. How wide, how long, how high is the Creator? Believe me, this temple we have built could never contain Him—yet these swaddling clothes do!

(praying) Oh, God, I love You and I thank You for this! I am utterly unworthy of Your holding me, and keeping me, as You have these many years, and here I stand, holding You! You are here with us now! Tell Job that I, too, know that my redeemer lives . . . and breathes, and laughs, and cries, and *(cooing to Jesus)* gracious, that was pretty loud! Yes, it was! Okay, let's give You back to Your mommy now.

I have held holy God in my own unholy arms. Can He love me that much? How about you, Jerusalem? How will you embrace your Savior? Will you reject Him if "this isn't the way you pictured it?" *(falling to her knees)* Father! Help us to accept You, that You might accept us!

SHEPHERD
by Jean W. Beasley
Christmas Portraits

Hallelujah! Glory to God on high! "Glory to God" . . . that's exactly what they said, exactly. I can never forget it as long as I live! I was scared to death—and so were the rest of them—don't let them kid you. I didn't want to breathe, for fear they'd take notice of me, or take offense, or something. Well, how were we to know? I cursed our luck for being caught in the middle of them like that, for we know no ordinary man can live through such a thing. Oh, but it was no accident! No! They came specifically to talk to us—oh, yes, they did! "Do not be afraid," the great angel said, and then, suddenly, we weren't—"Do not be afraid, for I bring you tidings of great joy that shall be unto all men." And then, this is the truly miraculous thing, I knew what they were saying. I mean, of course I heard it, but in my heart, *I knew.* "You will find a babe wrapped in swaddling clothes." The Messiah!

Why us, you might wonder? Why a bunch of smelly shepherds? Well, didn't King David, also a shepherd, teach us the nature of our God in his psalm, "The Lord is my shepherd, I shall not want"? God loves a *shepherd*! You may scorn me, but don't scorn your Messiah! I had not dared to really even hope, not once, not ever. And yet, there was my great Hope, a baby, born into the same squalid life I lead! That night, God sent His angels to break my heart, and they did; and they gave me a new one that same instant.

But I urge you to experience this yourself—understanding is no substitute! I don't understand it all—but I went to Him. I left my sheep—can you appreciate that? I left all I had in the world to look Him in the face! To touch Him!

Brothers! Angels will forever sing Jesus' praises! Can you hear them now? Praise God, the star still points the way—see it? Worship Him! Don't concern yourselves with—with yourselves! Can it be; is it that you have sacrificed, tithed, prayed, kept the law so exquisitely well that you are too good to meet God? He has come to you—are you now too good to go to Him? God was not too good to be born in a stable, and we few shepherds were not too good to kneel in one! Or are you not good enough, is that it? You have no offering prepared for Him, and you have heard that wise men kneeled at Jesus' feet and showered wealth upon Him? Yes, yes, true—but can you put Him off long enough? Do you plan to someday, somehow, measure up, and then meet Him as His equal? How can I make this real to you, brothers? God's own angels invited this poor shepherd to Jesus' side, and I—worthless as I am, I, myself, was all He wanted.

~

A REMEMBRANCE
by Matt Tullos

Christmas Portraits: Nicodemus

A dramatic moment for a hanging-of-the-green service

When I was still a young man, I heard the wonderful story of the birth of this baby called Jesus of Nazareth. I heard about the angels singing from the heavens, fearful shepherds, a miraculous star, gifts from strangers. He was born in a stable and placed in a feeding trough. Quite a humble beginning for a king. I also remember the terrible hunt by a wicked king, in fear of his own fate, seeking to kill the baby . I can still hear the mourning of young mothers who were stripped of their most precious possession.

Years later, I heard of the miracles and teachings of this same Jesus. My irresistible desire to meet this man led me to a home where He was staying. It was a windy night when I heard Him speak those words, "For God so loved the world that He gave His only begotten Son that whosoever believes in Him shall not perish but have everlasting life."

Lord, You are right to symbolize our eternal gift in Christ with the evergreen tree. What a beautiful reminder! What a fragrance! It also reminds us of another tree. One not so beautifully adorned as this. A splintered beam that held the broken, beaten, crucified body of God's son. I will never forget the face of our Beloved at that moment in time. I was on holy ground. I saw my sins and the price that was paid to make me clean. To make me—like this plant—ever alive!

You Gave Us Your Son

by Matt Tullos

A reading for Christmas worship

Leader: We needed hope.

Congregation: You gave us Your Son.

Leader: We needed forgiveness.

Congregation: You gave us Your Son.

Leader: We needed to learn how to pray.

Congregation: You gave us Your Son.

Leader: We needed to know that You understand our hurts.

Congregation: You gave us Your Son.

Leader: You gave us everything we will ever need when

Congregation: You gave us Your Son.

Leader: And so we remember that in that small village called Bethlehem you made life worth living, the load lighter, and hope a reality, when

Congregation: You gave us Your Son.

THE GRAND ANNOUNCEMENT
by Peggy Nikkel

Cast: *Angel #1, Angel #2*

Angel #1: Holy, holy, holy, is the Lord of hosts. The whole earth is full of His glory.

Angel #2: Holy, holy, holy is the Lord God Almighty, who was, and is, and is to come.

Angel #1: You are worthy, our Lord and God, to receive glory and honor and power, for you created all things, and by Your will they were created and have their being.

Angel #2: Gabriel returned from his mission to the earth. It has begun.

Angel #1: Then it is true. I had heard that the Son was going to lay down His glory and take up the humiliating form of man.

Angel #2: The Son has done this. Very willingly, I might add. The Almighty Father has such love and compassion for His creation that He would send nothing but the best as representative of the love and salvation He has offered to man.

Angel #1: But I don't understand. I can't comprehend how the Son could lay down all of His glory and honor for such a lowly task.

Angel #2: I doubt that anyone will ever understand the magnitude of His love.

Angel #1: But who on earth will praise and glorify His wonderful name?

Angel #2: Very few.

Angel #1: Will He know any honor or exultation during His mission on earth?

Angel #2: No, none, except His final ultimate victory.

Angel #1: If He knew all of this, why did He go?

Angel #2: Because He loves His Father's creation — but more than that, He loves the Father and wants to please Him.

Angel #1: Oh, it shall be a grand announcement! Just to see the wonder and surprise as the multitude of the heavenly host suddenly appears in the palace of Caesar Augustus . . .

Angel #2: No announcement will take place in the palace; it is to be witnessed by a handful of lowly shepherds. You have been chosen to accompany the multitude.

Angel #1: Glory, glory to God. How holy is His blessed name.

(Lights out. A spotlight center stage reveals Angel #2 with arms outstretched. The heavenly host surrounds him, including Angel #1 who is looking at Angel #2 with wonder.)

Angel #2: "Do not be afraid. I bring you good news of great joy that will be for all the people. Today in the town of David a Savior has been born to you; He is Christ the Lord. This will be a sign to you: You will find a baby wrapped in cloths and lying in a manger."

Heavenly Host: "Glory to God in the highest, and on earth peace to men on whom His favor rests."

A SONG IS BORN
by Guy Maddox

The story behind "O Little Town of Bethlehem"

Setting: *A small desk and a single chair, vintage 1860's. On the desk are paper, an inkwell, and a dip pen.* **Phillips Brooks** *wears black shoes, black trousers, and a clergy shirt with tab collar.*

Narrator: Christmas 1868, draws near. Phillips Brooks, popular Rector of the Episcopal Church of the Holy Trinity, Philadelphia, is in his study.

Brooks: *(Sits at desk as lights come up; rises and thinks out loud.)* The four years of war had taken a heavy toll on many of us. Those war years were no time to travel. Daily we faced news of the dying, as well as the care of the widowed and the wounded. Many able-bodied men were away in uniform. When the war ended in the spring, I was bone-weary. My heart was heavy from so much suffering and so many shattered families. As year's end approached, I was exhausted. I took leave of the church and sailed for the Holy Land.

I had never been there before. As I walked where my Lord Jesus had walked, I felt strength returning. I saw the very mountains He had climbed. Around the Sea of Galilee where He taught and healed the multitudes long ago, I walked. Here Jesus had welcomed the children. He loved them, and they gladly came to Him.

Children—today they still have such an interest in that matchless Jesus. There are so many children here in our church. But they are city children—and Jesus was a Man of the country. My dear children of our Sunday School face the jam of a hundred carriages at any corner and horse carts beyond number on our bustling streets. They see so many people, and all in such a hurry, all crowded into busy Philadelphia. How can I help them understand the life of our Lord?

That Christmas Eve, in His land, we borrowed horses and traveled the six miles from Jerusalem to Bethlehem, on a nearly deserted road. As evening came on, we rode through the shepherds' field to our Savior's birthplace. Approaching, I saw no streetlights, no crowds. It was just a tiny town. Stars sparkled in the sky as we drew near. I could barely distinguish the outlines of houses in the darkness and the stillness. On that Christmas Eve three years ago, I could easily imagine a tiny town 1800 years ago—a tiny town, and a quiet night, and empty streets. *(Sits at desk again.)*

Midst all the bustle and hurry we build around the Christmas season in our city, how can I help these city children of Philadelphia understand that tiny town—that quiet community—*(Piano begins to play single notes of the melody, slowly.)*—that backwater village where God visited us? So much noise around the children in our city, but how silent there in Bethlehem!

How can I make real today what happened so long ago? How can I explain to my children the setting of that first Christmas? That first Christmas in Bethlehem—in the little town of Bethlehem—in the still town of Bethlehem—*(begins to write; piano has picked up tempo so melody is recognizable.)*—with its deep and dreamless sleep—beneath the silent stars—silent stars once split by everlasting light. That—little town—of Bethlehem—*(lays down pen, stands with paper in hand, and begins to sing "O Little Town of Bethlehem," when piano reaches beginning of stanza. Brings in congregation to reprise stanza 1 at close.)*

The Baptist Hymnal, 1991, No. 86.

IN THAT SAME COUNTRY
by Jeff Warren

Imagine for a moment if Jesus was born tonight

At Christmas we celebrate the birth of our Lord, as it took place a long time ago, a long way away. We see this miracle birth through the filter of 2000 years with knowledge of Christ the original witnesses did not possess, and perhaps a more romantic picture of it than reality allowed them to see.

But imagine for a moment that it did not happen then—that for some reason God waited—and it happens—it happened—well that it's happening even now in a place not far from here.

If you eat at the Waffle House you probably know Maggie. She's a waitress. She's from Glenville, Kentucky, a white dot on a blue highway. Maggie came to Atlanta about five years ago after her divorce became final. She left all the things she grew up with in that town. She wanted a new life. Driving south, she pictured herself working as a secretary/receptionist in a high-rise downtown, wearing attractive business clothes, riding up in an elevator every morning.

But none of her interviews panned out. One matronly interviewer told her brusquely that she sounded too country to work answering the telephone, and Maggie quit interviewing after that. She went back to being a waitress. It's what she knew; she'd been doing it since high school, and nobody had ever cared what she sounded like.

It was a disappointment, but she's known a few of those. She's loved other men since her husband. She really did love the first one. She grieved when he left her, as if a part of her had died. She

decided not to do that anymore—not to let herself love like that. But the world is such a lonely place. Sometimes she holds a man—never loving him, because she knows he'll be gone soon—but pretending that he loves her, trying to imagine what it would be like if someone did love her, if someone did love Maggie. But she knows it's pretending.

Jake works the same shift Maggie does. He's the cook. He was an Army cook, but he's better than that sounds. He was put out of the Army. I don't know why—maybe for cooking too well. He lives a solitary life; doesn't talk much; trusts no one.

Jake prides himself on his work. Flipping an egg or grilling a steak, getting it right is real important to him. Funny as it may sound, he feels a kind of power in front of a griddle. It's the only place where he's in control. He can work ten orders in his head and on the grill at the same time. Jake puts on a show and people notice. When you're hungry and he's cooking, he matters, he's significant—at least until the shift is over. And isn't that what everyone is looking for—significance?

Lester walks in carrying a cardboard box and takes a seat at the counter. From the box to the counter top he trots out his wares: ceramic knick-knacks, festive and collapsible metallic ornaments, miniature brass watering cans and tea kettles, oversized coffee mugs with little stuffed animals inside. One holds a moose with a rack of stuffed antlers hanging over the brim. Lester stacks all the stuff neatly in front of him, handling each piece delicately as if a caress might enhance the value. It's all junk.

Maggie pulls three dollars from her apron pocket and buys the moose.

"It's cute," she says. "Do you have a box for it?"

"Lady," Lester says, "If I had room in my car to carry boxes for this stuff, I'd trash the boxes and add more merchandise. I don't do gift wrap, I'm sorry."

So much for service after the sale. For Lester, his car is his hotel, his office, his warehouse. And the New Year season is a cash cow; you milk it for all it's worth. Abundant life?—he's never heard of it.

Seven homeless men gang outside the door. Two of them rush inside: a stooped, skinny guy, kind of old, and a guy with a beard. They stand by the cash register in threadbare coats and overstretched stocking caps. They smell bad. Lester pinches his nose and stares down the counter in their direction.

"Whatya want?" Jake asks point blank.

"Three cheeseburgers, three orders of hash browns, and three coffees to go," the bearded one says.

"What are ya paying with?"

The man produces a wadded red bandanna and empties its contents on the counter: one gray button, two subway tokens, four dollars and fifteen cents in change.

"That ain't near enough," says the cook.

The man looks down at the money and turns toward his friend.

"We gotta take somethin', " the stooped one says. "They probably been travelin'. May be hungry. May be needin' somethin'. I don't wanna go empty-handed."

Lester climbs off his stool and strides down toward the men. "Say, gents, what's the emergency?"

"We've been told there's a child born near here, this night," the bearded man begins. "We're goin' to see him, and we wanna take some food with us—for his folks. They're just in town; didn't go to no hospital. Reckon they might be needin' somethin'"...some help."

"Say, sad story! Where is the little family?" Lester asks.

"In a boarded-up service station down by the interstate. That's what we was told."

"Oh yeah? Who told ya?"

The bearded man's face hardens. He draws himself up tall and looks straight ahead. He says nothing. The bent man raises his eyes from the floor and looks across the counter. For a moment his eyes meet Maggie's, but he instantly looks away. "Angels," he says softly, looking at nothing.

"Angels! Angels?" Lester sits on a stool and laughs out loud. "Boys, I've heard some tales of woe, but that beats all. Angels," he says and laughs some more. "I bet they had wings to flap around with too, didn't they—little haloes and gold harps to plunk on. Or did they come out of a bottle? Yeah that's it, a bottle—a bottle of wine!" Lester slaps his leg and laughs himself breathless. Jake is laughing too. Lester recovers himself somewhat and starts in again. "Were they dressed in white robes? Did they sing to ya?"

"Yeah," the stooped man says, still staring, "Music like I've never heard before. One sweet voice like a momma's lullaby, growing into an army of voices. It echoed like the ocean. It shook the ground. It trailed away like a marching song and made me wanna sing, too. It made me wanna sing, too! I can't remember the last time I wanted to sing— about anything."

His eyes are suddenly full. Tears break and trickle down his cheeks. He grabs the counter with one hand, covers his face with the other, bows his head, and sobs. His whole body shakes while Lester stares speechless and Jake stands mesmerized, leaning over the counter, his hands planted solidly with the coins and tokens between.

"Give them what they want," Maggie says. "I'll pay the difference."

Jake looks at Maggie, hesitates, turns to the griddle, and methodically begins. Maggie moves closer to the homeless men. "Tell me what else the angels told you," she says.

The bearded man smiles gently and nods. "They said it was good news they were bringing. That this baby is a Savior. His name is Christ, the Lord. And they gave us a sign too: they said we would find him sleeping in a cardboard box, on a mattress of shredded newspapers."

Lester laughs some more. Jake finishes the order and Maggie helps him put it in take-out boxes. They don't know if the Lord's parents like sugar or cream or both, so they pour a large black coffee and another with cream, and send some sugar packets and empty cups so they can work it out the way they like it. Maggie also caps a large cup full of orange juice, thinking the Lord's mother might rather have that.

When it's all ready, Maggie rings it up, sweeping the coins off the counter and into the till, making up the difference out of her apron pocket. The stooped man gathers the packages in his arms.

"Thank you, ma'am," he says. "This means more than I can tell ya." He looks like he could cry some more.

"Don't forget your change," Maggie says, and stuffs the bandanna, the tokens, and the button into the old man's coat pocket.

The bearded man picks up the coffee, smiles and says, "Thank you, miss. Thank you for your kindness." The two men turn to leave.

Just finished repacking his trinkets, Lester spins round on his stool. "Say, guys, you said this baby is a Savior—a Savior of what? What's He gonna save ya from?"

The bearded man pauses in the door. "I think maybe, mister, to save us from that." And he points out the front of the restaurant. The two rejoin the gang of men outside and move off down the street, leaving Maggie, Jake, and Lester staring after them into the darkness.
"What did he mean by that?" Jake asks.

"Who knows?" Lester says. "Well, there goes a free meal for a bunch of drunks. Maggie, you should have been somebody's momma."

Maggie says nothing. She stares out the glass where the messenger pointed. She sees the lights of the city, cold and distant in the dark. She sees a neon sign on the motel across the street: vacancy. She sees her own reflection, small and dark and distorted in the plate glass. She runs and grabs her coat.

"Now where you goin', Maggie?" Jake hollers from the other end of the counter. "We're gonna have half the U.A.W. in here inside of ten minutes."

"I'm going to see that baby," she says. "I'll be back in just a little while, but I gotta go see Him. What if He is the Savior, Jake, sent from God? Well, I just realized I've been lookin' for Him for a long time—most all my life. Well, I just gotta see Him, that's all. I just want to look at His face."

ISAAC AND JESUS
by Matt Tullos

The sacrifice of two sons and two fathers

Cast: *Narrator #1, Narrator #2, God, Abraham, Isaac*

Narrator #1: What shall we say to these things?

Narrator #2: How shall we respond to a love so incredible?

God: Abraham—

Narrator #1: God called

Abraham: Yes, Lord? I'm here. I was just about to finish up for the day.

God: In the morning I have a task.

Abraham: Certainly Lord. What do You want me to do? Tomorrow is a full day, but I'll make it my first priority.

God: It is concerning your son Isaac.

Abraham: Oh, I understand. You're probably wanting me to teach him how to hunt. I'm sorry. I've been putting that off for some time now.

God: No, Abraham.

Abraham: If You are worried about his behavior, let me assure You that he's just going through a stage.

God: Abraham—

Abraham: Oh, excuse me. If anyone should know about stages it would be You. You certainly have seen all my stages. By the way, have You heard him sing? He's not only a child of laughter. He's also quite a musician!

God: Abraham, listen!

Abraham: Oh I almost forgot. You had a task for me. Something for Isaac, wasn't it? I will gladly do whatever You ask me to do.

God: Take now your son, your only son—

Abraham: Isaac. That's my boy! Who'd have ever imagined that Sarah at such a old age would—

God: Take him to Mount Moriah—

Abraham: So it's time now for him to learn about worship. You want me to—

God: —offer him as a sacrifice.

Abraham: I'm sorry I don't think I quite heard that last —

God: Offer your son as a sacrifice.

Abraham: Offer Isaac. . .

Narrator #2: Abraham's mind raced. He stood in the presence of God as a chill ran down his spine.

Abraham: Offer Isaac as a sacrifice? Why? Lord, I have riches. I'll offer a thousand oxen. But my son. Isaac? He's my only son. In truth he's all I have. The only truly amazing gift that I was given from You. I don't understand. God—please don't make me understand! Not me—I can't do that. Lord, I love You with all my life! I would die for You. But to kill my only son? No I will not! I cannot! God! Why?

Narrator #1: Not sure of himself,

Narrator #2: Abraham retreated to his house. He didn't sleep. He wouldn't eat. Bargaining through the night with a God whose voice was not heard throughout that night of torture,

Narrator #1: grief,

Narrator #2: agony,

Narrator #1: and despair.

Narrator #2: I'm sure he cried,

Abraham: "My God. My God! Why have You forsaken me!"

Narrator #1: He must have begged—

Abraham: "If it be Your will, let this cup pass from me!"

Narrator #2: But amazingly, he resigned

Abraham: "Not as I desire but as You desire."

Narrator #2: Before dawn, Abraham rose from his pillow which was dampened with tears, hitched his mule, wakened Isaac, and made his way to Mount Moriah.

Abraham: If He leads me through the darkness
If He leads me through the darkness
If He leads me through the darkness
I'll go with Him
With Him
With Him, all the way

Abraham: "Stay here,"

Narrator #1: he said to his servants.

Abraham: The lad and I will go up and worship.

Narrator #1: So Abraham took the wood that he had split for the alter and laid it on Isaac—his only son.

Isaac: My father—

Abraham: Here I am son.

Isaac: We have the fire and the wood but where is the lamb?

Abraham: My son, God will provide the lamb—

Narrator #2: A thousand thoughts must have swept through his mind as he held the knife; thoughts that were crushing, thoughts that dug into the core of his soul.

Abraham: God, why do You demand this? I know that You are real. I've heard Your voice. I love my son. God, I love him so! Please Lord! This act! Such a horrible shameful act. But Lord I heard Your voice. Those words, I can't escape them. My soul is rotting to the core but I can't drown out Your words with my deep anguish. Let me die! Let me die instead. Why! Why must I . . .

He approaches his imaginary son. He lifts the imagined knife as he trembles and weeps. Then as it comes down—his arm freezes in air.

Narrator #1: The test was over but it was only a foreshadowing event of another Child who climbed the hill with the wood for the sacrifice on His back.

BLIND BARTIMAEUS
by Ragan Courtney

Ragan once again expresses profound truths through biblical characterization

I awoke every morning when I felt the warmth of the sun on my face, but I never saw that silver line on the horizon when the dark canopy of night was pried from the edge of the earth. I never saw the slow majestic journey of a red sun rumbling up a lavender ladder to its golden pinnacle. I never saw light dance on the sea. I never saw my mother's smile. I never saw my father's dark eyes twinkle. I never saw red.

As a child, I could see; but my mother told me of a childhood illness, a high fever, and then the blindness. I don't remember seeing. I don't remember color. All my days seemed the same every day of my colorless life. I would fold up a colorless mat, eat colorless food, be led to the market to ask seeing people to put colorless coins in my colorless cup.

Sight was not something that I missed because I could not miss what I did not remember. I did know how some things looked, though. I knew that my mother was soft and round, and her face was smooth with little crinkles around her eyes. My curious fingers had felt her face...often. Sometimes she would stop what she was doing, and let me look at her face with my little boy hands. (How did I know that they were probably dirty?) Sometimes she would brush me away with a "Not now, Bartimaeus! I'm busy." And I would listen to familiar sounds and rhythms and pats that would tell me that she was making bread, or sweeping, or cleaning dishes.

Sometimes at night before I went to bed, she would take me up on our flat roof where it was cool, and let me sit on her soft lap engulfed in plump comfort. I would sit breathlessly as she described what she saw...a sky turning from dark blue to purple, a crescent moon "like the shape of God's nail clipping," she would say. And the evening star...a point of light. I wondered what a star was. There had been those nights when my mother held me and softly spoke of the beauty of all the stars that I would touch her face near the familiar lines around her eyes, and feel tears. I knew that she wept for me, her poor blind boy. To me, stars and my mother's eyes were probably alike.

Not wanting to be a burden on my family, I did the only thing that there was for me to do—I begged in the market...for years. Being blind is not that different from being invisible. People tend to ignore you and walk past you, or stand within hearing distance and carry on conversations as though you were not there. I have learned a great many things about the human condition by simply sitting in the market in Jericho and listening. It was while there that I first heard of the teacher from Nazareth. I heard Him called everything under the sun from blasphemer, teacher, charlatan, to Messiah. All that I knew was that whoever He was, He certainly got people excited!

Then one day I heard them talking about the fact that He, the Nazarene teacher, was coming to Jericho. My curiosity to see Him grew and grew until it became an obsession. I waited for days straining my ears for evidence of His coming.

I got to my post as early as I could each day. I did not want my mother to lead me home in the afternoons because I was afraid that I would miss Him, and I had heard enough about Him to know that if He could do even part of the things that people were saying about Him...heal cripples, turn water into wine, feed thousands when He only had a few loaves and fishes, and—wonder of wonders—give the blind their sight, I had to meet Him. No, see Him! I had to see!

I heard them coming. They were still a good distance away, but it was as if the old walls had caught their sound and had reverberated the news to me that Jesus was on His way. As the crowd grew noisier, I knew that He was getting nearer and nearer. The excitement was building in me until I felt that I would scream. I had to run to find Him; me, a blind man groping down winding alleys trying to find a miracle. That would never work, so I began to call out to Him because I realized that in all that crowd of people following after Him, He might not see me. How would He know that I needed Him if I did not let Him know? So I began to call His name...I called louder and louder. "Jesus. Jesus. Over here. I'm over here. Help me! Help me please. Jesus. Jesus!"

I must have gotten someone's attention, because the people that had moved into my area next to the little niche in the wall where I begged told me to be quiet. They said I was making too much noise. I was making too much noise? It sounded as though all of Jericho was screaming and calling out for something or other from Jesus. I called louder, "Jesus, Son of David, have mercy on me!" Someone pushed me down, then threw my cloak over me to shut me up. I felt a sob rise from the depths of my soul. The crowd must have blocked me from seeing Him, and I missed my chance. He had passed me by. I could hear the crowd moving on...then they stopped and grew quiet.

I heard a voice say, "Call him here." Then I felt someone poke me, "Get up," they said. "Jesus is calling for you." And lying there in the dust, hope was reborn. With a jump, I was to my feet. I threw aside my cloak, and many hands directed me, leading me right to the Healer.

"What do you want Me to do for you?" He asked.

"I...want...to...see...again," I answered.

"Go your way; your faith has made you whole," He said.

I was stunned. Suddenly, there was a painful burst of light as I stood there accepting my miracle. There were thousands of bright, glittery things floating in the air, and right in the center of them was...this man. He smiled, and I knew that it was Jesus. I later found out that the thousands of glittery things were merely dust moats, but to me they were dazzling. They still are. The most ordinary, everyday things look like a miracle to a blind man who has just received his sight. I looked at this One before me, at His dusty sandals, His worn robe, His beard, His mouth. "So this is a grin," I thought. I looked at His nose. "Bigger than I would have guessed," I thought. I looked at His eyes. "Stars," I thought, and they were looking at my eyes that...were...looking...back at Him. And that is when I began to follow Him.

WHAT IS LOVE?
by Don Blackley

The following two sketches can be used effectively in children's worship

Good for puppets.

Cast: *Mrs. Foster, classroom teacher; Bobby, Chad, Kari, Ruth, four students*

As the scene opens the students are coming into the classroom and getting settled. They are chatting until the teacher arrives.

Kari: Ruth, did you see that beautiful sweater that Sheila had on? I just love it!

Ruth: Yeah, and I'd love to have the money that it took to buy that sweater.

Chad: Bobby, psst, Bobby. Is she looking at me?

Chad: Kari — is she looking at me?

Bobby: Kari? She doesn't even know you're alive!

Chad: When I saw her at the bus stop this morning she spoke to me.

Bobby: No kidding, what did she say?

Chad: She said, "Hey fella, move, you're standing on my lunch sack." I think she likes me. She may even love me.

Bobby: Love? Oooo Chad, lover boy!

Mrs. Foster enters the classroom.

Mrs. Foster: Good morning children.

Children: Good morning, Mrs. Foster.

Mrs. Foster: This morning as part of our English study I want you to complete this statement, "Love is . . ." *(all children squeal and giggle).* Kari, you may be the first to speak.

Kari: Love is . . . love is that funny feeling in your tummy when you see someone you really like a lot.

Chad: *(talking to Bobby)* See Bobby, I told you she noticed me!

Bobby: You're sick, sick, sick . . .

Mrs. Foster: That was very nice Kari. What do you think Ruth?

Ruth: Love is when you feel on top of the world because all of your friends like you and you've done really well at school . . . and your parents haven't grounded you . . and your cat just had kittens . . . and you just feel good, and . . .

Mrs. Foster: That's quite enough Ruth. Let's see what Chad has to say.

Chad: I really don't know what to say Mrs. Foster. I use that word so much I'm not sure if I know what it means. I love to ski in the mountains. I love my parents. I love my dog. I love to walk in the rain and squeeze mud through my toes . . . but I still don't know what love is!

Mrs. Foster: Thank you Chad. I was going to say love is never having to say you're sorry, but somehow that seems a little stupid now.

Bobby: Teacher, I think love is something you do. It really doesn't matter what you say with words. If you don't show by your actions that you care about someone what different does it make? My dad shows me he loves me by fixing my bike. My mom lets me know she loves me by taking care of me when I'm sick and feeling rotten. I really think love is something you do!

All puppets face the audience and speak together.

All: Let us not love in word . . . but in deed. 1 John 3:18. It's in the Bible! *(They exit.)*

JESUS WAS A FRIEND
by Don Blackley

Good for puppets.

Cast: *Nicodemus, Woman at the Well, Child*

Scene opens with three characters entering and singing together the first verse of "Jesus Is All the World to Me" (The Baptist Hymnal, 1991, No.184).

All Characters: "Jesus is all the world to me, my life, my joy, my all; He is my strength from day to day, without Him I would fall: When I am sad, to Him I go; no other one can cheer me so; When I am sad, He makes me glad; He's my friend."

All three puppets remain in place. The other two watch the speaker.

Nicodemus: Hi, I'm Nicodemus. I'm a religious leader of the Jews. A lot of my fellow leaders did not like what Jesus was teaching. Probably because it made them realize they were not pleasing God. So I was afraid that when I would go to meet Jesus, He wouldn't want to have anything to do with me. Was I surprised! He took the time to meet me one night. And He told me the most wonderful things about how I could go to heaven when I die. He took the time to be my...my Friend. After knowing His friendship, I told everyone I knew about His wonderful love.

Woman at the Well: He became my Friend, too! And I really needed a friend. You see, I didn't have anyone who wanted to be seen with me. That's why I was out there by the well getting water in the heat of the day! Because at least then I didn't have to hear their whispers about me. I didn't have to see the other women shove past me as if I weren't there.

So it was a real shock when Jesus came by the well and asked me for a drink of water. In the first place, I was a Samaritan. Jews didn't talk to Samaritans, especially a Samaritan woman like me. You see, I had been married five times and was really looked down on in my community. But He didn't condemn me. He just told me the truth. He befriended me, and I needed both His truth and His friendship!

Child: We had heard about this famous man who had been doing miracles all through the land. And my friends and I wanted to get close to Him and touch Him. But we also knew how things usually worked around important people. Once an important military leader came into our village on a large white horse. Even though we knew it was dangerous, we tried to run alongside that huge animal and reach out and touch the brass stirrup as we ran. All that got us was a big headache. Just as we ran up close, one of his foot soldiers saw us coming and batted us away with the sweep of his arm as if we were flies. So when we tried to work our way up close to Jesus, we weren't surprised when some of His followers collared us and drug us back away from the Master Teacher. But we were amazed when Jesus scolded them for treating us that way! Not only did He let us gather around Him, He sat down under a tree and took the time to tell us some stories. He wasn't too busy or too important to be my Friend. And I'm just a little guy! You'd better believe that we told our families and everyone we knew about how this important preacher was our Friend!

All: "Go home to thy friends, and tell them how great things the Lord hath done for thee," Mark 5:19. It's in the Bible! *(Characters exit.)*

I AM AMERICA
by Matt Tullos

A call to repentance

Cast: *Seven Readers*

Reader #1: I am a nation berthed from a yearning to breath free. I am freedom's shore. I came hundreds of years ago to find a haven where I could worship my God.

Reader #2: I found hunger, disease, and fear. I suffered torturous winters and sweltering summers, but the walls of a dictator no longer consumed me. I was free, and the freedom that I felt was worth the struggle. I died a thousand deaths to keep my freedom.

Reader #3: I was seized by ship, hunted like a wild animal across the barren beaches of my eastern coast. I was beaten, hanged, and buried but not defeated. Never defeated...

Reader #4: I was brought here not by choice. I was shipped to this land by men who bought and sold me like cattle. A slave...I had no choice. I had no ownership, but my heart dreamed of a day when freedom would sing my name. I lived only for the promise of the fiery chariot that would take me to a land of true freedom. And now after centuries of struggle and destitution I, too, am this nation. Once kidnapped by it, now a part of it.

Reader #5: I heard of the millions being slaughtered in gas chambers and concentration camps, and ruthlessly sought to destroy the villains who would commit such atrocities. I am a hero. I had mercy upon those who had no mercy on me.

Reader #6: I have seen the scandal, humiliation, triumph, and assassination of my leaders. I have longed for freedom and yet have abused the very tools of its making. I have killed the innocent, murdered the wise, and ignored the poets of each generation. Still my heart has a hope that has never diminished. A hope that was rooted on my day of birth. I have pledged my life, my fortune, and my sacred honor on that hope that I will be free. Will I seek not only peace and freedom, but also the Author of peace and freedom? Only God can say, for it is He who must be sought, and if I do not seek Him, I will never know.

Reader #7: I am Lincoln, Washington, Jefferson, and King. But I should never forget that I am also Lee Harvey Oswald, Charles Manson, and Al Capone.

Reader #1: I will only rise if I am willing to fall—

Reader #2: —to fall to my knees—

Reader #3: —and recognize the God who brought me here.

Reader #4: I am the best and the worst of man.

All: I am America.

CARRY THE LIGHT
by Matt Tullos

Cast: *Paul, Israelite, Shadrach, Lazarus, John, Corrie, Lottie. Could use with* **Puppets.**

Paul: I was walking on the road filled with righteous indignation! I was right. I was sure of it! I had the answers and they were foolish dreamers who were leading away a multitude of stupid believers. The road to Damascus... But then the miraculous light, the unmistakable light, blinded my doubt and left me forever changed.

Israelite: The pillar of fire was lifted high above us. Like a constant message that the very presence of God was near. Every night—every long and desolate night, we were forever changed by the light!

Shadrach: We were left for dead in a furnace so hot that men perished from it's glow. But this fire seemed almost frigid to us. It was as if it didn't even exist. But what we did feel—what shined brighter than the furnace was our companion— the forth man in the fire! The Son of God. We were forever changed by His light!

Lazarus: The tomb had been opened. My tomb! Cold in the grave for days and yet I woke to an incredible light—not the kind of light that's produced by the morning sun or a lantern. No—this light was so powerful that it sent a pulse through my decaying body. So miraculous that my weeping friends were overcome by unbelievable, miraculous joy! I was dead. Yes. But then made alive again by this light! Jesus Christ! I was forever changed by my Friend, my Savior, the Light of the World!

John: I saw Him once more. Not as a man. But as King of Kings! His hair and his head were white like wool—as white as snow— and his eyes were like blazing fire. His feet were like bronze glowing in a furnace. I fell to my face and was forever changed by His light! The First and the Last—the Beginning and the Ending.—the Living One!

Corrie: I went through ten months in a concentration camp. My father died after ten days. My sister—after ten months of imprisonment. But we had seen the Light of the World. What others meant for harm, God has used for my good. I have grown closer to that Light. I am forever changed!

Lottie: Too small to go to China, some said. Too weak. Too frail. But I had the Light of the World within me. I went to China! I lived and died in China. But not in defeat. Not in despair. The light was carried and God's light will never be snuffed out. We are forever changed by it!

John: For once you were in darkness!

Shadrach: Absolute despair

Corrie: But now you are in the light of the Lord.

Lazarus: Live as children of the light.

Lottie: No one lights a lamp and puts it in a place where it will be hidden,

Paul: You are the light!

All: Let your light so shine!

Scripts for Ministry

THE HUNGER WALL
by Darlene Tullos

Cast: *Two couples, **Doug** and **Debra**; **Lloyd** and **Linda**, and **Narrator**. Could use **Puppets**.*

Props: *Two large boxes, strong enough to sit on*

*An imaginary wall is in the middle of the stage, dividing it into two sides from the view of the audience. **Doug** and **Debra** are on one side; **Lloyd** and **Linda** are on the other side. A box is placed downstage on each side of the stage. **Doug** and **Debra** enter first.*

Doug: Wow, look at this place, Debra. It looks great. All these big trees are beautiful.

Debra: The trees have fruit on them, too. I've never seen such pretty fruit.

Doug: Look, here's a box, too. I wonder what's in the box? I guess it's for us.

Debra: Let's open it, Doug. Oh, this is so exciting!

They bend down and mime prying the top off the box.

Debra: Can you get the lid off? It must be on there tight.

Doug: (*straining to get it off*) Uuuuugggghhh! (*The lid pops off—they both look excited at what they see.*) Look at all of this food. Can you believe it? (*They mime taking the food out of the box.*)

Debra: Peanuts and popcorn, and fruit-at-the-bottom yogurt, my favorite!

Doug: Pizza, potato chips, broccoli and cheese soup. Wow!

Debra: Let's see what else is under here. Turkey and dressing, chicken, bacon and eggs, and Coke Classic. I don't know what to eat first.

Doug: Look over there, Debra. It's a TV!

Debra: We can munch and watch TV at the same time.

Doug: Sure am glad somebody left all this for us!

Doug and Debra freeze in their positions by the box. Lloyd and Linda enter on the other side of the stage.

Lloyd: Kind of a desolate looking place, huh? It looks as if it hasn't rained in months.

Linda: I'm getting a little bit hungry. How about you?

Lloyd: Yeah, I could use a bite to eat.

Linda: Well, I see some fruit up on those trees, but it's sort of shriveled and dried up. We probably couldn't reach it anyway.

Lloyd: Hey, Linda. Look over here. It's a box. Wonder what's in it?

Linda: Maybe there's food inside. Let's open it.

Lloyd: You think we should?

Linda: Sure. Here, help me get the lid off.

They kneel down by the box and begin trying to pry off the lid. The lid pops off--they both peer inside.

Lloyd: Nothing!

Linda: There's nothing in the box. What a disappointment. I wonder what we should do now?

Lloyd: I don't know. Let's think about this for a minute.

*Lloyd turns the box over, and they both sit on top of it, assuming a "thinking" position. They freeze. **Debra** and **Doug** unfreeze.*

Doug: Hey, Deb. It's Thursday night! Grab some of that popcorn, some pizza, and a couple of Cokes, and let's watch Bill Cosby. (*sings theme song from The Cosby Show*)

Debra: Great idea, Doug. This is so much fun.

Doug and Debra turn their box over. Doug mimes turning on the TV. They sit on the box and begin to mime eating, using their books as trays. They can also react to the show and ad-lib softly. After a moment, Lloyd and Linda unfreeze.

Linda: Listen, Lloyd. Do you hear something? (*They strain to hear.*)

Lloyd: Yeah, but I can't tell where it's coming from.

Linda: (*looking over the imaginary wall*) Sounds like it's coming from the other side of that wall.

Lloyd: Maybe they have some food that they would share with us. I'm really hungry, aren't you?

Linda: Yeah, I'm hungry, too. The wall is too high to see over. (*thinking*) Hey, maybe if I climb on your back, I could see over the wall and see if they have any food.

Lloyd: Okay, that's a great idea. If you see any food, try to get their attention.

Linda gets up on the box to climb on Lloyd's back.

Lloyd: Careful, now. Are you set? Okay, I'll walk slowly over to the wall, and you look over. Okay?

Linda: Okay.

Lloyd walks over to the wall. This could be very comical. Debra and Doug are still watching TV, eating and laughing.

Linda: (*as Lloyd gets up to the wall*) Wow, I don't believe it! It's incredible! (*She stares over the wall for a few seconds.*)

Lloyd: (*straining to hold her up*) What is it? What do you see?

Linda: (*speaking very fast*) Huge fruit trees with every kind of fruit you could imagine, and a big box filled with food—pizza, popcorn, turkey and dressing—

Lloyd: Do you see any people?

Linda: (*looking hard*) Yeah, I think I do. Hurray, we're saved!

Lloyd: See if you can get their attention.

Linda: Hey, over there. Can you hear me? We're really hungry. We don't have any food.

As Linda begins to yell, these lines are done over her lines.

Doug: Do you hear something? (*begins looking around*)

Debra: Yeah, Doug, I do, but just very faintly. Where is it coming from?

As Doug and Debra start to look over at the wall, about the same time Linda falls off Lloyd's back. Doug and Debra catch only a small glimpse of Linda. Lloyd and Linda freeze.

Doug: Did you see that? It looked like someone peeking over the wall.

Debra: I wonder who it was?

Doug: I don't know.

Debra: Hey, Doug. I've got an idea. Maybe if I climbed up on your back, we could see over the wall and find out who is over there.

Doug: Okay, that sounds good. Climb up on that box. That will be easier.

Debra climbs up on Doug's back, and Doug walks over to the wall in much the same way that Lloyd did in the previous scene.

Debra: (*upon reaching the wall, looking down at Lloyd and Linda*) Aahhhh! (*She gasps.*) This is horrible! I can't look. Put me down. (*Doug puts her down.*)

Debra goes to the box and covers up her face as she continues to remark about what she has seen.

Doug: What's wrong, Debra? What did you see?

Debra: Oh, it was awful. The people over there are so sick and hungry. It makes me sick at my stomach. I wish I'd never seen them. It's an awful sight. Don't look at them, Doug. It will just make you feel guilty.

Lloyd and Linda unfreeze and begin yelling from their side of the wall. They get more intense with each word.

Lloyd: Could you please help us? We have nothing to eat.

Linda: Could you share some of your fruit with us? We're so hungry.

Lloyd: We know you are over there. Please help us.

Linda: We're sick and hungry. Please listen. We need your help.

These lines begin to overlap, and Linda and Lloyd repeat these lines and ad-lib as we hear Debra and Doug talking.

Debra: Listen to them, Doug. They are yelling for help.

Doug: It's not our fault that they have nothing to eat.

Debra: I wish they would leave us alone!

Doug: Let's just turn up the TV louder and maybe we won't be able to hear them. (*mimes turning up TV*) Grab some more of that food over there.

Debra mimes picking up some more food and then comes and sits by Doug, as Lloyd and Linda continue to yell louder and louder. They also mime beating on the wall. Debra and Doug sit cramming food into their mouths but look miserable doing it. When Doug speaks the first word of the next line, Lloyd and Linda freeze with arms up as if beating on the wall.

Doug: (*loudly*) You know, Debra, I'm not having fun any more.

Narrator: Now what use is it, my brothers, for a man to say he has faith if his actions do not correspond with it? Could that sort of faith save anyone's soul? If a fellow man or woman has no clothes to wear and nothing to eat, and one of you says, 'Good luck to you, I hope you'll keep warm and find enough to eat,' and gives them nothing to meet their physical needs, what on earth is the good of that? (*James 2:14-16 paraphrased*)

"Let us stop just saying we love people; let us really love them, and show it by our actions" (*1 John 3:18, TLB*).

A Father's Heart
by Rick Shoemaker

Lord, when did it happen? We used to be so close. I remember when she was three or maybe four. We went out for lunch at McDonald's. She wanted to be the waitress and take Daddy's tray to the garbage can after we ate. After she emptied the trash, she came running back with her eyes bright and that grin from ear to ear. "Daddy, Daddy! I can spell garbage! P-U-S-H!"

Those years passed by too fast. School started and my little girl was growing up. That first day of class when I held her tiny hand and she waved bye-bye, she thought I had abandoned her. That afternoon she was so excited when she got a smiley face on her first paper for good behavior. She always seemed to love school then.

What year was it? Second grade? She was going to have her school picture made. I came home from work to see the living room covered with all sorts of clothes. Her poor mother was exasperated. "What seems to be the problem?" "Daddy, I can't decide what skirt to wear with my blouse for my school picture." I said, "It doesn't make all that much difference, honey. The picture will only be from the waist up." "Nuh uh! I'll show you. It says right here on this paper: Tomorrow pictures will be taken of the entire student body!" Well, she's blond; took after her mother. Cute, but a little spacey.

And then came junior high. Seems like she didn't need me so much then. Not as many memories. One I'll never forget, I decided I needed to lose weight, again. She and I were driving some place and she offered me a drink of her Diet Pepsi. "No thanks." "Take a drink; it's good." "I'm not really thirsty." "Oh, Dad, it's Diet Pepsi. It's only got one calorie and you probably won't get it if you take one sip!" We had some wonderful times. But now, we don't talk anymore! We don't laugh anymore. We either build walls or throw bricks.

Ever since that night she came home drunk. Maybe I didn't handle it very well. But I knew that boy was a bad influence. He was a smooth talker, but I saw his disrespect for my daughter. After that party, I had it out with him. He dumped her and she's never yet forgiven me for that, I don't think.

It seems the only time she speaks to me is when she needs money for something. Maybe it's my fault. I know I work long hours, but college is coming up; and with her braces and higher insurance rates... I want so much for her to know how much I love her. I know I make mistakes. I sometimes yell. And maybe I am too strict at times. It's just that I know the pitfalls. I fell into a few when I was her age. And I die inside when she makes the same mistakes.

Maybe I understand how You feel, Lord, when Your children shut You out. I don't think I ever knew just how much You loved me until I became a father. And Lord, forgive me for my rebel spirit. I know how much You love me and I know how much I love my little girl. Help my daughter understand how much we love her. Lord, that wall of anger, of pride, of stubbornness that stands between my little girl and me, I want that wall to come tumbling down. Show me what must be done.

Narrator: *(optional)* Are there walls that stand between you and those who love you? Isn't it time they come tumbling down?

SORRY, I'M ON VACATION
by Melinda Yessick

A comical reminder that the work of the church doesn't end while you're gone

Cast: *Husband* and *wife relaxing in lounge chairs in tourist attire and suitable props. Could use with* **Puppets.**

Setting: *Relaxing in lounge chairs in tourist attire and suitable props*

Him: Now, this is the life!

Her: I can't believe we finally got away for a little rest and relaxation.

Him: No phone, no meetings, no alarm clocks!

Her: Speaking of meetings, did you tell the chairman of deacons you'd miss the deacon's meeting this week?

Him: Nah, they'll figure it out. Besides, Jeff knows where I am. I hope he remembers he's teaching my Sunday School class. Anyway, if they ask, he'll tell them I'm on vacation!

Her: It is good to get away from that telephone. Hey, did you pay the phone bill before we left?

Him: It's not due until the 15th. I'll do it as soon as we get back. My arms are tingling a little, and I just want to try and relax. Remember, I'm on vacation!

Her: They're tingling because of the marathon golf game you played today. It takes a lot out of those old arms to dig up that much turf! They probably thought you were digging a trench instead of teeing off!

Him: Very funny! I guess it has been awhile since I've played. Maybe that's why I'm a little tight across my chest.

Her: Well, what's on the schedule tomorrow?

Him: Maybe we can tour that historic church we passed by coming into town. Let's plan to eat something plain and simple tomorrow. I guess I've got indigestion from tonight's dinner.

Her: Speaking of church, did you send in our tithe?

Him: No, I'll do it when we get back. Give me a break...I'm on vacation!

Her: Well, I just know the pastor encouraged everyone to be faithful during the summer months.

Him: Yeah, yeah, I know. But right now I'm trying to relax...I'm on *(both saying)* vacation!

Her: Honey, are you OK? You don't look like you feel well.

Him: I must have overdone it today. I'm really starting to hurt in my chest.

Her: Do you think it's something more serious than soreness from your golf game? You know, it could be your...

Him: Heart? I was considering that...Ooh! Honey! A sharp pain just shot through me. Oh, dear God...

Heard over the public address system, deep voice.

God: Sorry, I'm on vacation!

THE SERVANT OF GOD
by Gerald Morris

Studying Amos? Try this educational dramatic interpretation

Adapted from: *Amos 7:10-17*

I can't think of anything that interferes with the genuine ministry of the Lord more than the ranting of these self-proclaimed prophets. A servant of God has enough to do keeping up with the needs of his flock without having to spend his time trying to counter the silly arguments of doomseers, or (as I call them) "Doom-Dooms."

And I do mean silly arguments. Have you ever noticed that none of their beliefs ever has any real basis? "As the Scripture says..." they all begin, and then they cite some obscure passage from Deuteronomy that could be interpreted in a dozen different ways, but they seem to feel can only be interpreted in their way. And their interpretation is always a fantastic interpretation that—wonder of wonders—no one in thousands of years of Scripture interpretation has ever come up with before. Not two weeks ago I spent over four hours trying to reassure a widow that the sky wasn't falling on her head just because one of these idiots said so. She had heard this prophet preaching and was afraid that the country was lost and she might as well hang it up right now. And this is one of the finest, most God-fearing ladies I know.

This last one—the one whom she had heard, the one who had nothing better to do than to terrify little old ladies—was the worst. First of all, he wasn't from around here. He was from way down south, probably from one of those cults that you hear about down there, the ones who shave their heads and wear funny clothes and eat bugs or whatever. So he's suspicious right off. I mean why do you suppose this gentleman isn't preaching down home? Probably because they know him down home.

But the thing that really burns me is that he's preaching to strangers, saying that God sent him to tell them off. What does he know about the people he's preaching to? When he tells a widow that her sins are going to destroy her country before she can say Jehoshaphat, does he know that widow? Does he know that two years ago she buried her husband of 30 years? Does he know that her eldest daughter ran away from home and became a prostitute at Gilgal, that her only son won't speak to her, and that in spite of all this, in spite of the worst pain that a mother can know, she still faithfully worships the Lord and never once has complained, never once has doubted? Of course he doesn't know! He hasn't lived beside her for years, worked beside her husband, watched her babies grow up. I have. I know. But he doesn't.

I never did convince her that this wandering cultist was a fraud. It made me so angry that I hunted him down and confronted him. It didn't take long. I told him that he was more welcome at home than he was here and sent him off. He went, of course—I don't mean to brag, but I do have some authority in these parts—but he showed his true colors before he left, spouting off insults about my wife and family. What surprises me is that anyone ever listens to these fanatics.

I've been priest at Bethel for a lot of years now, and I'm finally getting some recognition. There's even been talk among some of the worshippers here of putting some of my teachings down in a book—the Words of Amaziah—so that I'll be remembered after I'm gone. If that ever happens, I hope someone remembers how I got rid of this infernal nuisance, this fig-picking, self-proclaimed prophet from Tekoa, this Amos. That's how I hope I'm remembered.

THE TREASURE HUNT
by Douglas Crawley
Sketch based on Matthew 6:19-21

Cast: *Doug and Chip*

Chip comes in with metal detector, totally oblivious to others. He can walk over to congregation, orchestra, etc.

Doug: Chip, what in the world are you doing now?

Chip: I'm hunting for buried treasure!

Doug: Well, there's no buried treasure here.

Chip: I wouldn't be too sure about that. I'm picking something up right now. Praise the Lord! It's *gold*!!

Doug: Chip, that's not gold. It's a *tuba (or something)*.

Chip: Are you sure it's not gold?

Doug: It's not gold.

Chip: Well, it's the same color as gold.

Doug: It's *not* gold!

Chip: Maybe it's fool's gold.

Doug: It's not fool's gold.

Chip: It sure fooled *me*.

Doug: So why are you looking for buried treasures?

Chip: I want to be wealthy.

Doug: Why do you want to be wealthy?

Chip: Don't you ever watch TV?

Doug: Well, sometimes.

Chip: The rich guys have all the fun. You know, cars, *girls*, houses, *girls*, boats, *girls*, motorcycles,

Doug: I get the idea.

Chip: *Girls*

Doug: You know the old proverb, Chip, "Money can't buy happiness."

Chip: Maybe it's just not on sale, yet.

Doug: It never will be. You see, God's word tells us that *real* treasure can't be found in material possessions.

Chip: Say *what*?

Doug: Money, houses, even gold can't last forever. Lots of things can happen and when you die, well you know the old proverb—

Chip: "You can't take it with you."

Doug: That's right.

Chip: Well then, what am I going to do with this? *(holding up metal detector)*

Doug: Well, the Bible tells us to lay up treasures in heaven.

Chip: I don't think the range on this baby will reach that far.

Doug: No, Chip. You won't need that for these treasures. I'm talking about things like charity, kindness, and sharing God's love.

Chip: Those are *treasures*?!?

Doug: That's right. Only the things we do for God's kingdom last forever, and they bring *true* happiness and fulfillment.

Chip: Hey, I may just sell this *(refers to metal detector)* and donate the money to charity.

Doug: That's the spirit. Say, Chip, does that thing *really* work?

Chip: Are you kidding? I've already found 68¢ today.

Doug: I've got an idea. I'll give you $10.00 for the metal detector and you can give *that* to charity.

Chip: It's a deal.

They exchange.

Doug: That reminds me of an old proverb "Prosperity is the reward of the righteous." *(tries to locate something with detector)* Hey, wait a minute! This thing doesn't work at all. But you said . . .

Chip: I said I found 68¢. I didn't say it *worked*. You know that reminds *me* of an old proverb.

Doug: What's that?

Chip: "A fool and his money are soon parted."

Chip leaves counting his money.

Worthless Words
by Melinda Yessick

Cast: *Nine Readers They stand in groups of three: 1,2,3/ 4,5,6/ 7,8,9.*

#1: Good morning!

#2: Good morning!

#3: No, it's not a good morning. I'm tired.

#4: How are you today?

#5: Fine. And you?

#4: Fine, thanks.

#6: No, I'm not fine. I'm discouraged.

#7: Good to see you.

#8: Good to see you, too.

#9: No, it's not good to see you. You hurt me!

(#'s 1,2,4,5,7,8 step forward)

#1: We see with our eyes, but we are blind.

#4: We touch with our hands,

#5: But we are unfeeling.

#7: We speak with our mouths,

#8: But our words are empty.

(#'s 3,6,9 step forward)

#3: I've been up all night with a sick child.

#1: I didn't notice your eyes.

#6: I've lost my job.

#4: I thought you had resigned.

#9: You've been gossiping about me.

#7: I didn't think you would ever find out.

#s 1,2,4,5,7,8: And they will know we are Christians by our love

#2,5,8: By our love

#1,4,7: By our love

All: Yes, they will know we are Christians by our love.

#'s 1,2: "Open my eyes that I may see

#'s 4,5: Glimpses of truth

#6: Thou hast for me

#'s 7,8: Open my ears that I may hear voices of truth

#3: Thou sendest clear

#'s 4,5: Open my mouth

#6: And let me bear

#'s 4,5,6: Gladly the warm truth everywhere"[1]

#'s 7,8: Open my heart

#9: And let me prepare

#'s 7,8,9: Love with Thy children everywhere.

All: Amen.

[1]"Open My Eyes, that I May See," The Baptist Hymnal, 1991, No. 502.

DO WHAT?
by David Roberts

A reading that addresses the challenge of obedience

Cast: *4 Men, side by side, facing audience*

1: There were thousands of them.

2: People were everywhere.

3: At least 5000 of them were men,

2: And you know men are always hungry.

1: They had followed us along the shores.

4: It's not our fault.

1: And now it was time to eat.

2: But guess what,

4: None of those stupid people brought any food.

1: And now our rabbi has just told us to feed them.

3: Uhh, we got a problem.

4: Send them all to McDonald's.

2: There's not any out here.

4: Well then, send them all to town.

2: I've already suggested that, but the rabbi said for us to feed them.

3: Yeah, right.

2: No, I'm serious, that's what He said.

4: Do you have any idea how much that will cost *(starts figuring)*.

1: Maybe we misunderstood Him.

2: No, He said for us to feed them.

4: That's gonna take more than any of us could earn in 8 months.

3: Well, it's not our fault they followed us around the lake.

1: Yeah, couldn't they tell that we were trying to get away?

4: I bet not a single one of them would ever pay us back. We can't afford this.

1: It's not fair, this was supposed to be a retreat with our rabbi, not some kind of mission project.

3: Yeah, even if we did have that kind of food or money, do you know how long it would take us to pass it all out?

2: I agree, it's an impossible task. You go tell Him.

1: No, then He'll start questioning our faith again.

3: Faith, what's faith got to do with it? We've got thousands of hungry people out there. We don't need faith, we need tons of food and lots of help.

4: Maybe we need to get back into the boat and leave.

3: Yeah, this isn't our responsibility.

1: Now wait a minute, we all know that this isn't our fault, we all know that it's an impossible task, but He did ask us to do it, so at least let's give it a try.

3: All right, maybe Father Moses will drop some manna or something out of the sky.

4: Or some money.

1: Let's see if we can find some crackers or something, just so He'll know we tried.

Men take a minute to mingle with front rows of audience, asking if anyone has any food.

2: Well, did anyone find anything?

3: I found this kid with a sack lunch. It's got, let's see, five pieces of bread and two pieces of pickled fish.

1: Pickled fish!

4: I get the bread.

1: No, we aren't gonna eat it ourselves. We are gonna take it to the rabbi and show him we tried.

3: He already knows about it, in fact he wants us to get all these people to sit down.

2: Why?

3: I think he's going to feed them.

1: One sack lunch?

2: This is getting embarrassing.

4: I'm getting back in the boat.

Men turn their backs to the audience—pause—then face audience again—acting as if each is holding a large, heavy basket with both hands.

1: What has Jesus asked you to do

2: That you thought was impractical,

4: That you thought you couldn't afford?

3: Has He asked you to fix a problem

1: That wasn't your fault?

2: Has He asked you to care for people

4: You don't even know?

1: We each came home that day,

3: All twelve of us,

2: Carrying these baskets of leftovers.

4: And these baskets are always reminding us that nothing,

2: nothing,

3: absolutely nothing . . .

All: is impossible with God.

I Can Be a Friend
by David Ward

Great sketch for childhood education!

Cast: *Wendy, Sidney, children's group. Could be done with Puppets.*

Setting *Wendy on stage telling Bible story*

Wendy: Good morning boys and girls. I want to tell you a story about Philip. A long time ago, there was a Eunuch riding down a dusty road in a chariot.

Sidney: *(enters)* Hold it! Who knows what a chariot is?

Wendy: *(adjust this response to answer)* Well, it is like a wagon with big wheels, pulled by a team of horses.

Sidney: Before you go on, what is a Eunuch?

Wendy: He was an official sent by his queen to buy things and make friends.

Sidney: What did Philip have to do with all of this?

Wendy: Philip was a preacher, and God told him to go meet the man riding in the chariot.

Sidney: Wasn't the man reading the Bible?

Wendy: Yes, he was reading from the Book of Isaiah, and he didn't understand what he was reading.

Sidney: Did Philip understand what he was reading?

Wendy: Yes, and the man asked Philip to explain it to him. *(pause)*

Sidney: Well, go on, don't let me stop you.

Wendy: So, Philip got into the chariot with the man and told him about Jesus and how much Jesus loved him. The man asked Jesus to be his Savior and Philip baptized him in the first river that they came to.

Sidney: So, Philip really enjoyed telling others about Jesus!

Wendy: Yes, Philip really loved God.

Sidney: I'll bet our friends here like to tell others about Jesus.

Wendy: I'd say you're right. Hey, I want to teach you a verse about being a friend. Ephesians 4:32 says, Be kind to each other. Say it with me.

(Repeat until adequate)

Sidney: You've been so good today, and we really enjoyed visiting you again. We'll see you again soon. Bye. *(exit)*

Wendy: Bye *(exit)*

WHO DO YOU KNOW?
by Matt Tullos

Motivate your church to reach the unchurched

Cast: *Game Show Host, Stan, Marv*

Host: Good Morning and welcome to *"Who Do You Know"*—brought to you by *(name of your church)*. This is the game show that asks the question, "Who do you know?" I'm your host *(name)*, and here's our current champion, from *(name of town)*—Stan Grover. Let's give him a hand. *(Applause)* Good Morning! Are you ready to play???

Stan: You bet!

Host: That's the spirit, Stan. Here's the question—for 25 points. Who's the pastor of *(name of your church)*?

Stan: Oh, Great. I'm a member!!! It's uh . . . uh . . . *(name of pastor). (bell)*

Host: That's correct! *(applause)* Good job, Stan! Way to go! That brings us to the bonus round—

Stan: Oh wow! I can't believe it!

Host: Now listen closely.

Stan: You bet, Pat!

Host: Who do you know that doesn't go to Sunday School in and the surrounding areas?

Ticking sound.

Stan: That's a toughy . . . Uh . . . Uh . . . I can't believe it . . . I'm drawing a blank. Uh . . .*(bell)*

Host: Sorry Mr. Grover. Times up.

Crowd groans.

Host: I can't believe it! The answer was obvious. Almost too many to count. George, your postman. Harry, your accountant, and then there's Mary—how could you forget your own secretary? And how about that old friend of yours—Mark????? And then there's that kid in your Boy Scout Troop—Joey!!

Stan: Shucks!

Host: And here's what you could have won! Tell'em Marv!!

Marv: You *could have* won eternal rewards—contentment that you did what God called you to do—a million smiles—and a wonderful growing church.

Audience groans.

Host: But guess what Stan? You still have time left in the bonus round!

Audience applauds and cheers.

Stan: Fantastic!!!

Host: So don't give up. We'll see you next week on *"Who Do You Know?"*

Marv: This is one game you can play at home. Who do *you* know that doesn't go to a Sunday Morning Bible Study. You never know when the trumpet will sound, When you hear it, the game's over!! Don't miss the prize!

Applause.

CALLED TO CARE
by David Roberts

A creative dramatic object lesson suitable for worship or fellowship occasions. Study directions carefully and have fun!

*There are **Six Actors**, each with a letter on their front and back. These can be poster boards worn "sandwich style" or large letters sewn on white sweat shirts. The letter should be large enough to be seen by the audience. Could be done with **Puppets**.*

Actor	Letter on front	Letter on back
#1	C	S
#2	H	E
#3	U	O
#4	R	L
#5	C	A
#6	H	T

In the stage directions, #1-b means that actor #1 has his back to the audience. #5-f means that actor #5 is facing the audience, etc. The order in which actors line up always starts with stage right.

Actors are lined up, shoulder to shoulder, facing the audience in numerical order. (#1-f, #2-f, #3-f, #4-f, #5-f, #6-f). The letters should spell "CHURCH."

#3 We are the Church.

#6: The Body of Christ.

#1 Created by Christ to make a difference.

#4 To make a difference in this world.

#5: We gather to worship.

#2: And we scatter to minister.

Before and during the next line, the actors rearrange themselves into the following order: #6-b, #3-b, #1-f, #5-b, #4-f, and #2-b.

#1: Of the many things we are called to do . . .

#4: Perhaps the most important is our call to care.

Actors should now be spelling "TO CARE." Be sure there is a gap between #3 and #1.

Before and during the next line, the actors rearrange themselves into the following order: #2-f, #3-f, #4-f, #6-b. Actors #1 and #5 are hiding behind the line so that their letters do not show.

#3: We have been called to care for those who hurt.

Actors should now be spelling "HURT"

#2: "Blessed are the poor in spirit, for theirs is the Kingdom of heaven. Blessed are those who mourn, for they will be comforted." (Matt. 5:3, NASB)

Before and during the next line, the actors rearrange themselves into the following order: #4-f, #2-b, #1-b, #6-b. Actors #5 and #3 are hiding behind the line so that their letters do not show.

#4: And we have been called to care for those who need rest.

Actors should now be spelling "REST."

#3: *(Peeking head out between #2 and #1)* Come to me, all you who are weary and burdened, and I will give you rest. *(Matt. 11:28, paraphrased)*

Before and during the next two lines, the actors rearrange themselves into the following order: #4-b, #3-b, #1-b, #6-b. Actors #5 and #2 are hiding behind the line so that their letters do not show.

#5: *(Peeking head out between #3 and #1)* And we have been called to care for those who are lost.

Actors should now be spelling "LOST"

#2: (Peeking head out between #1 and #6). "For the Son of Man came to seek and to save what was lost."

Actors rearrange themselves into the following order: #1-f, #2-f, #3-f, #4-f, #5-f, #6-f.

#1: The Church, called to care for those who hurt.

The next three lines are spoken rapidly like a cadence.

#2: Ouch

#3: Ouch

#4: Ouch

#6: The Church, called to care for those who need rest.

The next three lines are spoken rapidly like a cadence.

#5: Ouch

#4: Ouch

#3: Ouch

#4: The Church, called to care for those who are lost.

The next three lines are spoken rapidly like a cadence.

#3: Help

#2: Help

#1: Help

#2: And who is this church?

Actors #1 and #3 line up behind #3, hidden from the audience. Likewise, actors #5 and #6 line up behind #4.

#3 & #4: You are

Actors rearrange themselves into the following order: #6-b, #3-b, #1-f, #5-b, #4-f, and #2-b.

#4: And you have been called.

ALL: To care!

LITTLE JOEY TEACHES SUNDAY SCHOOL
by Matt Tullos

Sunday School enlistment promotion sketch

Cast: *Marcy, Jacob, Joey, and Belinda. Could be done with* **Puppets.**

Try using adults to portray the following sketch. It was written to express the need for children's Sunday School teachers.

Marcy: Zaccheus was a wee little band
And a wee little band was he
He climbed up in a Sycamore tree—-

Jacob enters room.

Jacob: He's not a wee little band. He's a wee little man.

Marcy: He was a wee little what?

Jacob: A man! A wee little man!

Marcy: But if he was wee little, then he must have been a kid.

Jacob: Nope. He was just a short man.

Joey enters.

Joey: Hi Marcy, hi Jacob. Where's Mrs. Snodgrass?

Marcy: Mrs. Snodgrass said she wasn't going to teach our Sunday School class no more. She said she needed more smelloship with her own age.

Joey: What's smellowship?

Jacob: I don't think it's smellowship. I think she said fellowship.

Marcy: Well, what is smello—I mean fellowship?

Jacob: I think it's when you eat Reeses pieces, sing hymns, and talk about Jesus all at the same time.

Belinda: Who's gonna talk about Jesus with us?

Jacob: Yeah. Who?

Marcy: Don't everybody look at me!

Joey: *(raising his hand wildly)* Oh! Oh! I will.

Belinda: O.K.

Jacob: Whacha gonna teach us?

Joey: Give me a second.

Marcy: Maybe you should bite your nails. That's what my dad does when he thinks real hard.

Joey: I got it. Our Bible story today is about Jonah and the flood.

Belinda: Jonah and the flood?

Joey: See, God was gonna send a big flood storm and Jonah had to build a boat cause he was good and so he gathered up all the animals . . . all except the lions.

Marcy: What did he do with them?

Joey: He throwed them in a den.

Belinda: With a T.V. and a lazy boy.

Joey: No silly! They didn't have T.V.'s back then.

Belinda: Oh.

Joey: Anyway, Jonah's family threw him overboard and he got swallowed by a whale who spit him up on the shore at the end of a rainbow.

Jacob: That don't sound right. Grown-ups tell the story right.

Marcy: And they know how to make stuff outta fruit loops.

Joey: Then what are we gonna do?

Belinda: I want a Sunday School teacher just for our class. A grown-up one—

Jacob: I know what we should do. I know! Mrs. Snodgrass said that if we wanted something real bad that we should pray.

Belinda: Yeah!

Joey: That's right.

The children bow their heads and fold their hands in prayer.

Marcy: Here is the church. There is the steeple. Open the door . . . Jesus, where is our teacher?

Freeze

THE NEIGHBORS
by Christy Doyle

How do you celebrate Christmas?

Cast: *Two couples, Mary and Gary; Stephanie and Jason.* **Setting:** *A typical living room. Mary is looking out the window. Gary is reading a book.*

Mary: Gary, you would not believe the yard across the street. You know, Margaret told me that those new neighbors are Christians. You know . . . I don't think they are real committed Christians. How could they be?

Gary: What do you mean, Mary?

Mary: Well, their yard has so many Christmas decorations that . . . well . . . it looks like a tavern.

Gary: So . . . big deal. They like Christmas lights.

Mary: Gary, we're talking major lights here. Come here. Take a look at this.

Gary: Wow . . . I wonder how long it took him to put all those up?

Mary: Too long. Christmas should be a religious holiday . . . You know they have a Christmas tree that probably cost a fortune.

Gary: Mary, I miss having a Christmas tree.

Mary: Well, that's not what Christmas is about. You know they're are going to be so embarrassed if their pastor sees all those gaudy decorations.

Gary: I don't think they're gaudy. I think their house looks nice.

Mary: Yeah . . . in a worldly sense I guess it does, but I'm only thinking of them.

Gary: If you're thinking of them, why don't you go talk with them?

Mary: No! You know I hate meeting new people. I took me two years before I met the Mandels . . . Margaret was in K-mart and saw them buying Santa Claus Christmas paper.

Gary: What? Is Margaret in the FBI now?

Mary: Gary, she's only telling me because she's afraid for these people and their salvation.

Gary: Correct me if I'm wrong, but I don't think Santa Claus paper will send a person to hell.

Mary: Well, of course not . . . But it might make you forget entirely what Christmas is all about.

Gary: And what is that, Mary?

Mary: Why, the birth of Jesus.

Gary: So, do you really think Jesus would be upset with Christmas lights, trees, and Santa Claus? I think Jesus is the ultimate Santa.

Mary: Gary, that sounds almost sacrilegious. *(Looking out the window)* There's a big delivery truck pulling up in front of their house.

Gary: *(Mocking)* Oh no! Perhaps they're getting presents delivered!

Mary: Oh, Gary, you are not going to believe this.

Gary: What? *(He looks out the window. He reads.)* "Jesus is the reason for the season." Now, do you feel better?

Mary: Yeah, right. Could we have a more embarrassing sign in our neighborhood?

Gary: I thought that's what you wanted.

Mary: I don't want a big sign outside. That thing must be six feet high.

Gary: At least they are telling people about their faith. We're so holy . . . no one knows.

Mary: Jesus was a quiet man.

Gary: He didn't keep quiet about who He was . . . and He loved people.

Mary: Are you saying I don't love people?

Gary: No, Mary, but you do tend to judge people.

Mary: I can't believe you're saying that about me.

Gary: Mary, I just think you should consider what Jesus would say and think, not what you feel you should say and think.

Mary: Look at that. They're leaving the house with tons of gifts. I knew they were materialistic.

Gary: *(Looking)* I think they're coming over here.

Mary: Maybe we should pretend we're not here. Yes, let's hide, Gary.

Gary: Mary, I'm not going to hide from someone in my own home.

Mary: Great! Now I have to make small talk with complete strangers. What will I say?

Gary: Mary, you've never had a problem with finding something to say. (The doorbell rings. Mary opens the door.)

Jason: Hi, we're the Fords. We just moved across the street.

Mary: Hi! Merry Christmas. We've been meaning to come over and introduce ourselves.

Gary: Hi, I'm Gary and this is my wife, Mary.

Jason: Hi, I'm Jason Ford and this is my wife, Stephanie.

Stephanie: I always make Christmas candy, so I thought you might like some.

Jason: Excuse me if I'm being rude, but I notice you don't have a Christmas tree. We put an extra one in our bedroom. We'd be more than happy to bring it over.

Mary: Oh, no, I'm sorry. We . . .

Gary: *(Interrupting)* We'd love it! It's very thoughtful of you.

Stephanie: We're bringing these gifts down to St. Anthony's Hospital. If you don't have plans for tomorrow evening, we'd like to take you both out to dinner.

Gary: That's very thoughtful. We'd love it.

Jason: We'd also like to invite you to our new church. They have a special Christmas Eve service.

Mary: Thank you—we'd like that. *(looks at Gary)*

Jason: I hope my wife and I won't bore you to death. We've been out of the country for so long I can't imagine having a normal dinner conversation.

Gary: Oh, what country were you in?

Jason and Stephanie together: Africa.

Stephanie: Jason and I were missionaries for four years in a remote part of Africa. We were so excited about being back in the States where we could celebrate our Savior's birth in real style. Don't you just love Christmas?

Gary: We've never really been Christmas people, but I think you two can show us how to really celebrate Christmas —don't you, honey? (*freeze.*)

_____

PRODIGAL II
by Gail Blanton

Worship Feature: *At some time in the service* *before this feature, have read the parable of the* *Prodigal Son, Luke 15:11-32.*

Father is onstage obviously watching for someone, either using an imaginary window—perhaps over the organ rail—or from his porch, shading his eyes with his hand and looking into the distance. Suddenly he notices the audience and addresses them as if they are visitors to his home.

Father: Come in; come in. I'm glad to see you. Sorry if I seemed preoccupied for a moment, but I am so disappointed in my son. He's run off, you know. What am I to do with him? Some people may have thought it was a stupid thing for a father to do, but I did divide up my living between them—my two sons. I gave him his fair share, to do with as he pleased. Since then I have put no compulsory requirements on his actions and expected him to put none on mine. Of course he knew what I would like for him to do, what I earnestly wanted him to do. And I knew what he wanted me to do. It is hard to watch your child go when you want him to stay and you feel he is wrong. It is perhaps harder for your child to stay when he wants to go and he feels you are wrong.

So with sadness, but no hysteria, I let him go, also. First, because he wanted to go so badly, he felt he had to go. Second, because I knew he needed to learn a lesson, however painful. And I'll wait for him also. When he comes to himself, he'll be back. One son gone, one at home. One at home, one gone. Oh, I'll worry about him, watch for him from time to time. I probably won't have to wait very long, and at least he's not that far away.

Now that is one consolation, because he didn't go off to a far country like you might think. No, he's just right over there in the next field, just east of here. Poor boy. He's made himself miserable, I guess. Well, love is not love if it's forced. I'll come and watch for him again at the next break.

Right now, we're missing the party. Come on, rejoice with us; the celebration's in full swing! The calf is ready to serve and everybody's in a merry mood. And I know you're anxious to see the guest of honor. Oh, you won't even recognize my younger son! His looks like a prince. He's changed a lot, but then he's been gone—how long has it been? Oh, what does it matter? He's home...home! You can't imagine how happy we are. We were up all night talking. Who wants to sleep? We're much too excited and he's just—well, come on, we'll let him tell you how he feels. *(Starts toward exit, but turns and looks out "window" one last time.)* Take care you don't hurt yourself, son.

Exits.

DIAPERS AND VOLLEYBALL
by Matt Tullos

Who will serve?

Cast: *Pat and Alan (adult men),* *Narrator*

Props: *volleyball, two diaper bags*

Pat and Alan enter with volleyball in hand.

Pat: It's the Volleyball Monster!

Alan: You got it, pal.

Pat: Ready when you are...

Alan: Okay. We can take these guys!

Pat: They might be a little bit taller than we are but we'll make up the difference with our speed and agility.

Alan: We've got to stay light on our toes.

Pat: Plus, we've even got better shoes.

Alan: All right, hand me the ball.

Pat: Hand you the ball?

Alan: Yeah, hand me the ball. I'm going to serve.

Pat: You're going to serve.

Alan: That's what I said.

Pat: But what about me.

Alan: You'll serve after me.

Pat: Now hold on. Don't you think we ought to put our best foot forward?

Alan: Of course I do. That's why I'm going to serve first.

Pat: But you have that little underarm serve thing that goes about two miles an hour.

Alan: Well, I admit your serves are harder than mine.

Pat: I'm glad that you can admit the truth.

Alan: But my serve actually stays inbounds.

Pat: Oh yeah?

Alan: Yeah! Sure you ace one every now and then, but by that time the party's over. It's 15-2 and we've been skunked!

Pat: Well at least we aren't humiliated by your ballerina approach, and the skip in your follow-through.

Alan: That's what you call finesse!

Pat: No, that's what I call embarrassing.

Alan: If you don't give me that ball right now, I'm going to call the whole match off.

Pat: Fine with me, Madame Butterfly.

Narrator: But serving to win is not about volleyball. It's about our commitment to Christ.

Pat and Allan turn around with a diaper bag instead of a volleyball.

Pat: Hey! It's our week in extended session. We're both in charge of the two-year-olds but I don't think I'm going to be able to help. The pastor's preaching on bitterness and I have a lot of it, so I think you're going to have to go it alone.

Alan: I'm sorry, pal. I have to leave right after Sunday School. You're going to have to serve this Sunday.

Pat: I'm not going to serve. I served two months ago and you weren't even a member back then.

Alan: I wouldn't have joined if I'd known that I was going to have to serve with you.

Pat: Thank you very much. What a fine example of Christian service you are.

Alan: You can talk all you want to about service, but I'm not going to serve this week.

Pat: Well I'm not going to serve, either. You've got to do it.

Pat: You serve!

Alan: No, you serve!

Pat: No, you serve!

Alan: No, you serve!

Pat: No, you serve!

Alan: And so the story goes, and where will it end?

Pat: Nobody knows.

Alan: Who will serve?

Pat: Not for athletic achievement,

Alan: Not for fame,

Pat: Not even for their own well-being,

Alan: Who will serve to share the good news of Christ?

Both: Who will serve to win?

WHERE ARE THE CHILDREN?
by Robert A. Allen

Sanctity of life

Cast: *School Principal, Teacher*

*The **Teacher** and **Principal** enter together, the **Teacher** carrying a stack of books.*

Teacher: My very own classroom; how exciting!

Principal: Yes, isn't it. I certainly hope you will have a wonderful year teaching kindergarten.

Teacher: Why shouldn't I? This is the day I've looked forward to for years. My very first day of teaching.

Principal: I remember my first day of teaching. It was right here in this very classroom. Thirty-two freshly scrubbed and expectant faces eager to learn.

Teacher: Thirty-two?

Principal: Yes, that was before we became so concerned about class size. You won't have nearly that many, I promise you.

Teacher: Oh, it really wouldn't matter. I'm just so excited to have the opportunity to mold these youngsters into useful contributors to society.

A bell rings.

Principal: I'm glad to hear you say that. Our school is very concerned about pursuing our social agenda, you know.

Teacher: That's exactly why I wanted to teach here. I have my lesson plans all prepared—"values clarification," "world citizenship," "alternative life-styles," "the environment," and "how to sue if you think you're being harassed."

Principal: Very good! Very good! And all politically correct, I'm sure.

A bell rings.

Teacher: But where are the children, sir?

Principal: Well, I'm not sure.

Teacher: Not sure? Aren't you the principal?

Principal: Yes, but, you see, I'm afraid there was an accident.

Teacher: A bus accident? On the way to school? Why didn't you say something earlier?

Principal: No, not on the way to school. In fact, it's been six years.

Teacher: Six years since the accident?

Principal: At least. And I'm afraid that means there won't be any children for you to teach.

Teacher: Because of an accident six years ago? You're not making any sense. Where are my children? Do the parents know their children aren't in school?

Principal: Yes, they're the ones who decided.

Teacher: Who decided what?

Principal: That the *children* were the accident.

Freeze.

WHO WILL SERVE?
by Matt Tullos

A call to ministry

Cast: *Two Readers*

Reader 1: When they close the doors and there's no where else to go—

Reader 2: When the abused child needs love that he's never felt before—

Reader 1: When the man who seemed to have it all, loses his home, his dignity—

Reader 2: Who will serve the people?

Reader 1: When Jesus call us to win the world,

Reader 2: and save that lost and dying man

Reader 1: from a drug,

Reader 2: a hurt,

Reader 1: or even a disease

Reader 2: that we don't quite understand—

Reader 1: Who will serve the people?

Reader 2: We have been content with programs, personalities, and thrills

Both: still—

Reader 1: a lost generation

Reader 2: is crying out of desperation.

Reader 1: "Wake up!"

Reader 2: cried the prophets. If you a *still* before the Lord, can you not hear their voices echoing from the past to where we are today?

Reader 1: Echoing into this room with our climate controlled conditions—

Reader 2: The empty man!

Both: Look to him!

Reader 1: The desperate woman!

Both: Look to her!

Reader 1: The hungry man no more than a mile away from this green house of religion.

Both: Look to him.

Reader 2: Jesus cries out— "Look to him!"

Reader 1: Who will serve?.

Reader 2: Not on committees, or in offices, or on boards, or even juries, *no*!

Reader 1: Who will serve to win?

Reader 2: Will we—reach out with more than out minds?

Reader 1: Will we reach out with our hearts?

Both: With faith for the future?

Reader 2: Who will serve?

Reader 1: Who will pour the water—

Reader 2: kneel—

Reader 1: weep—

Reader 2: and with the finest cloth that he possesses

Both: wash the feet of a lost generation?
Who—— will—— serve?

PRAYER INVESTIGATION
by Gail Blanton

You don't have the right to remain silent!

Cast: *Major Angel, P.I.; Woman*

P.I.: Excuse me, ma'am, I'm Major Angel, P.I.

Woman: Private Investigator? What do you—

P.I.: No, no. Prayer Investigator.

Woman: I see. Well, I'm really in a hurry.

P.I.: I only have a few questions and they're quite important. You're a suspect in a charge of gross negligence with intent to delay another's salvation.

Woman: I beg your pardon, young man. I would not ever delay anyone's salvation.

P.I.: I understand you're quite concerned about your brother becoming a Christian?

Woman: Oh, yes. I've witnessed to him, brought him to church, had the pastor go over—

P.I.: So of course you've prayed for him this morning before you left?

Woman: Well...no—as I said, I'm in a hurry today.

P.I.: Last night then.

Woman: Goodness, no! I was too exhausted. Church family night meetings, you know.

P.I.: Yesterday morning?

Woman: *(becoming irritated)* No, I don't think so.

P.I.: Last week?

Woman: Look, I'm really worried about my brother. Doesn't that count? I don't have to be praying for him every minute do I?

P.I.: No, you don't. You have the right to remain silent. Anything you do *not* say *can* and *will* be used against you in the court of God on Judgment Day. You have the right to an attorney. If you cannot afford an attorney, one has already been appointed for you—Jesus Christ the Advocate. You're free to go.

Woman: I know I'm free!

P.I.: You have the right to remain silent.

Woman: I know my rights! And my brother's!

P.I.: What about your obligations?

Freeze.

THE PRESS CONFERENCE
by Matt Tullos

Imagine, if you will–spiritual warfare through the eyes of angels!

Cast: *Angelic Journalist, Archangel Michael, Lieutenant Angel Josiah, Reporters 1, 2, 3, 4*

Extras: *TV Cameraman, Photographers*

*A **Journalist** begins the press conference as another actor appears as a cameraman. The **Journalist** speaks as if he is breaking into normal programming.*

Journalist: Good Evening. We have just heard that Lieutenant Angel Josiah and, of course, Archangel Michael are expected here in the briefing room to make a short statement, and to field any questions that the heavenly press might have about the recent escalation of spiritual warfare brought about by the evil princes of darkness. *(pressing his ear as if he was listening to a message from an earplug)* Now we are being told that the Lieutenant and Archangel should be here at any moment. There is a sense of baited anticipation as the angelic journalists wait. Many in this room feel that the Operation Return could happen any day now. Well, as you can see, the officers are now making their way to the podium. Let's listen.

*The platform features a large map and a TV monitor. The Christian flag is also on the platform. The **Angelic Officers** enter, dressed in white robes with medals pinned on them. As they enter from one of the choir doors, several **Photographers** approach the front, kneel down and begin taking flash photos.*

Michael: Ladies and gentleangels, members of the press. I have a short statement to read and then we'll take a few questions. Let's begin with the statement. *(reading)* We are aware that the recent spiritual battles have concerned and even frightened many mortals who are serving as foot soldiers. The Holy Spirit is actively working to comfort those men and women who are on the frontline. Let me stipulate that we are totally confident in the Lord. As our Commander-in-Chief has reminded us time after time—the battle is His. The enemy's strategy is spiritual terrorism which is totally useless as long as our soldiers rely on God's power and not their own. *(pause)* Now we'll allow a short time of questioning.

*The **Press** gathering immediately begins to barrage the platform with cries of "Lieutenant Josiah!, Lieutenant Josiah!" They wave their hands, pencils and pads, reminiscent of any press conference. After a moment **Josiah** recognizes **Reporter 1**.*

Reporter 1: What weapons are being used by the forces of darkness at this time? And can you elaborate on your strategies to overcome them?

Josiah: Basically, they're using the same weapons that they've always used. They're accusing Christians, attacking them with low self esteem, causing them to be angry with their spouses, tempting them to be unforgiving and bitter—you know. The same old stuff. Lately it seems they are escalating the use of media missiles and ground to air fear bombs.

*As soon as he finishes his answer, the hands of **Reporters** go up, as well as shouts for his attention.*

Reporters: Lieutenant! Lieutenant!

Josiah: Yes? *(He points to a **Reporter 2**.)*

Reporter 2: Some reports have speculated that the Antichrist is on Earth at this very moment. Can you respond to this speculation?

Michael: Lieutenant, let me answer that one. *(**Michael** approaches the podium.)* Let me first say that we are not privileged with that information. I can only encourage us to remember that our battle is not with flesh and blood. To speculate these kinds of issues will only distract us from our commission given to us by the Commander-in-Chief.

Reporters clamor.

Reporter 3: Could you outline where the major battles are occurring at this point in time?

Josiah: The battles ar so widespread that it's difficult to analyze, but let me highlight a few of the hot spots where tremendous fire fights, pardon the pun, are occurring. *(He uses the map.)* We are seeing great victories in Africa. As you know, an incredible revival of the redeemed forces are taking place there. Also in China, our victories have been miraculous! We've had reports that whole companies of redeemed forces are experiencing tremendous victories. It's also been reported that some companies are victorious despite not having a single sword! On the other hand, I'm sorry to say that some of our strongest troops are experiencing defeat. For instance, the forces of darkness are scoring major victories among the Christians of the United States. With the use of division missles and "holier than thou" grenades, the enemy has come close to dividing this company of believers. We can confirm that some soldiers have even ceased attacking the enemy and have started attacking each other. This is very discouraging especially in light of the fact that they have the most artillery and soldiers.

Reporters clamor.

Reporter 4: What has been the most successful means of defeating the evil forces of darkness?

Josiah: Certainly our forces have tried a multitude of methods. They have passed out literature to the enemy. They have produced TV shows to be broadcast in enemy territory. They have written new battle hymns. They have even dramatized the biography of our commander and chief. Using these techniques have not been as effective as the method that we've recommended using since the war began. Let me illustrate this strategy by showing you some footage that has been released by our military intelligence. *(**Michael** turns on the video player as **Josiah** continues by describing what we are seeing on the screen.)* Both segments here are from the recent conflict in *(town of your church)* The soldier's name is David Moore. He has over 30 years of combat experience. As you can see, this warrior is driving up to the prayer room—now he is entering—now he is sitting down and preparing to do battle through prayer—and now he commences to attack the forces of darkness. After one hour of intense

battle the forces of darkness were crippled by over ten direct hits. *(The video continues.)* Now this is private mortal Jared Stange. He's serving on the front lines in the battle of _____. As you can see, he's entering into enemy territory, _____ High School. Now watch closely as he pulls out his sword and storms into a P.O.W. camp and rescues a captive using not only his sword but also the weapons of prayer and love. These are two of the strongest weapons we have. Jared scored a massive blow to the plans and schemes of the devil. *(The video ends and **Michael** turns off the TV.)* I believe we have time for one more question.

Reporters clamor.

Reporter 1: What is the atmosphere as the commanders meet to discuss the war?

Michael: We are all excited about the ultimate victory that we are going to have. Commander Daniel, Captain Isaiah, Lieutenant Paul and well, all the joints chiefs of staff are prophesying a great victory. As our Commander has told us time and time again. The victory is ours! All we have to do is go out there and fight the battle.

Reporters clamor.

Michael: I'm sorry, that's all the time we have.

*More **Reporters** clamor as the two officers walk out of the room.*

Journalist: Well there you have it. Although Lieutenant Angel Josiah and Archangel Michael express some concern about the highly skilled yet unmotivated troops in America, he expressed that the victory as always is a fact. Praise God.

Now back to your regularly scheduled worship service.

Scripts For Fellowship

LEFTOVERS
by Melinda Yessick

Try this creative solo acting piece, which is an unusual, fresh, and comical look at Jesus feeding the multitudes

Cast: *Mother of Boy with loaves and fishes (costuming optional)*

Talking to her husband.

You've had a bad day? Oh, let me tell you about my day with your son! Embarrassed? I wanted to crawl under the nearest Judean rock!

We went out for the day and heard that the Teacher everyone's talking about, Jesus, was teaching outside of our town. I told your son that we'd pack a lunch. Well, you know I had to do laundry today, go for water, and then to the market. No time to bake bread. No worry though. We had leftover bread from supper last night, so I put a couple loaves in the basket along with a parcel of fish.

We're on the hillside and I'm visiting with Mary—the lady who lives down the road. Everyone's getting restless. We've been there a long time. It's hot. I turn to ask your son to bring the basket so that we could have lunch, when—poof! He disappeared! I was frantic! Such a crowd! I looked and looked. Mary helped and got her husband to look. Then she says, "Look down there, where the Teacher, Jesus, is."

Yes! Yes! It's him. But wait! What is he doing? Our basket, our lunch! He's giving to Jesus' followers *day-old-leftovers*!!! I was so embarrassed! Why didn't I get up early and bake fresh bread? If I had only known that he'd share it—with the Master! I just could have died! The rest of the day has just been a blur. When I finally reached your son, we couldn't find the basket. Doesn't matter, really. Luckily, we left before too many people knew where the leftovers came from. Didn't waste any time! As soon as I got my hands on that child, we left straight for home. I have a suspicion that they made fun of the lunch. We heard people cheering and clapping. People can be so cruel and sarcastic! It's a miracle—we got out of that crowd!

LOST AND FOUND
by Steve Phillips

An army! You lost an army?

Cast: *Pharaoh's Army Captain, Worker (female or male), Lady. Could also use with Puppets.*

A Lady is standing at the counter talking to the Worker.

Worker: I'm sorry. If I hear anything we'll call you.

Lady: Thank you. *(She exits.)*

Pharaoh's Army Captain has come in. He's wearing a gladiator-type hat and a toy gun.

Worker: Can I help you?

Captain: Me?

Worker: Yes. Have you lost something?

Captain: Yeah, but it's probably not here.

Worker: It might be. You'll never know till you ask.

Captain: Well, I don't know.

Worker: Go ahead and tell me your problem.

Captain: Well, I lost something, but it really wasn't mine.

Worker: Whose was it?

Captain: Pharaoh's.

Worker: You lost something that belonged to Pharaoh?

Captain: Yes. I mean it's gone. I saw it with my own eyes. I'm his most trusted army captain, but he'll never believe what happened. I'll never believe what happened. And I came here because I thought that maybe if I didn't really see what I thought I saw, you might know and...

Worker: Wait, wait! Let's just start at the beginning. Okay?

Captain: Okay.

Worker: Now, tell me what it is you've lost.

Captain: Pharaoh's army.

Worker: *(taken aback)* You've lost Pharaoh's army? How could you lose an entire army?

Captain: Well, I didn't really lose it. I mean, we were chasing the Hebrews and...

Worker: Hold it! *(writing)* Okay, you lost Pharaoh's army. *(not writing)* Okay, where did you lose it?

Captain: In the Red Sea.

Worker: *(writing)* In the Red Sea. *(not writing)* Why...I mean...never mind.

Captain: We were chasing the Hebrews and...

Worker: I was afraid of that. You mean the army was chasing the Hebrews and when they got to the Red Sea everyone fell in?

Captain: Everyone but the Hebrews.

Worker: What do you mean?

Captain: Well, the Hebrews didn't ever get in the Red Sea, and the army didn't really fall in. The Red Sea kinda fell in on top of them.

Worker: I knew I should have stayed in bed this morning. Now what exactly do you mean by the Hebrews not getting in the sea? Did they side-step your army, or take boats across, or what?

Captain: No, they walked across. *(He says "walked" so jumbled that the worker can't understand him.)*

Worker: They what?

Captain: *(clear)* They walked across.

Worker: *(laughs a little)* Do you mean to tell me that all of those Hebrews just walked across the Red Sea? On top of the water?

Captain: *(laughing with her)* No, no. It wasn't like that at all. The sea separated and they walked right across on the bottom. And it was dry.

Worker: *(looking around)* Hey, am I on Candid Camera?

Captain: No, it's the truth.

Worker: And I suppose your army tried to follow them, and that was when the water fell down and you lost your army.

Captain: *(surprised that she seems to know)* That's right!

Worker: *(ridiculing)* You're kidding!

Captain: No, I tell you. This is what really happened. You've got to believe me.

Worker: Sure, and I'm King Tut's mother.

Captain: Please, you've got to help me.

Worker: I'll tell you what. If anyone turns in an army, you'll be the first person I'll call.

Captain: *(truly thankful)* I'd appreciate that. *(starting to leave)* Oh, by the way, you're not going to tell Pharaoh, are you?

Worker: No, I promise I won't tell.

Captain: Thank you. *(He exits.)*

Worker: *(after he's gone)* I wouldn't tell that in a million years. *(She exits shaking her head.)*

LOST AND FOUND II
by Al Hunter

Hunter picks up where Steve Phillips leaves off

Cast: *Virgin (V); Lost and Found Worker (W); Shepherd (S); Father (F). Good for Puppets.*

V: Is this the Lost and Found?

W: *(pointing to sign)* Why yes, it is.

V: Well, you see I'm engaged and I had lost one of my dowry coins.

W: Had lost?

V: Yes, but I found it.

W: I see. Well, ummm, I mean, you don't need us then.

V: Oh, but I had to tell somebody. You see, it was like this: When I realized it was missing, I lit every lamp in the house. I swept every nook and cranny. And I found it! *(holding up a large silver coin)* Now, you see, I won't have to spend my life as an old maid. Isn't that great?

W: *(less than enthusiastic)* Yeah, great. Well, have a nice day.

V: You, too. *(leaves skipping along)*

W: Next. May I help you?

S: Well, I just wanted to share my joy with you. You see, I have 100 sheep. Yesterday I only had 99, but I searched all night 'til I found . . .

W: Sir, may I interrupt? Not you too? You see, we are the Lost and Found. *(points)*

S: That's right. But I just wanted to explain that just because I found my sheep, I don't think I should have to bring him to you. You see, when he was lost he seemed as valuable as all the other 99 to me. And now that I found him, I'll use all my power to keep from giving him up!

W: Sir, you're absolutely right. You just go tend your flock and have a nice day . . . Next. *(Shepherd bows and leaves expressing thanks.)*

W: And a good, good day to you, ma'am.

W: Let me guess. You lost something but now you've . . . *(nodding expectantly)*

F: Oh, it's more than that.

W: Good. How can I help you?

F: Well, you see, I have two sons. The younger said to me, "Dad, I'm not going to stay with the family business, may I have my inheritance now?" This really put me to the test, but what could I do? Even if I refused, he would have been so bitter he would have been just as lost to me. So I gave it to him.

W: And he lost it?

F: In a manner of speaking.

W: So you want me to put out a notice that . . .

F: Oh, no. I considered the money lost from the start, but it was a worthy investment. You see, he recognized the error and came home expecting nothing more. I could never have bought his love, so the money was worthless compared to having my son back. I want to invite you to the party!

SALT AND LIGHT
by Al Hunter

Biblical banter

Cast: *Salt and Light. Good for Puppets.*

Salt is seated on podium. **Light** *is coming down the aisle when he sees him.*

L: Salt! You crusty old seafarer. I didn't know you were going to be here today.

S: Light! You young whippersnapper. My, you're looking bright today.

L: Hey, man. I like your taste.

S: That's what I'm here for.

L: What for?

S: And who for.

L: Why four?

S: Therefore.

L: Therefore what?

S: To add taste.

L: Oh.

S: So you see?

L: Yeah, that's what I'm here for.

S: What for?

L: Therefore.

S: Therefore what?

L: Therefore, let's do our thing.

S: Look, you...

L: Not without light.

S: What do you mean?

L: You said, "Look." I just pointed out that you can't do that without light.

S: Oh, I see.

L: Because of light.

S: You know. . .

L: Yep!

S: Yep, what?

L: I was just agreeing.

S: Agreeing with what?

L: You said, "You know" and I was agreeing that I do. . .know.

S: You're trying to show me something?

L: That's what light's for.

S: Yeah.

L: So you're beginning to see!

S: Now if I could just teach you some good taste.

L: Hey, don't blame me that so much of our talk is based on seeing.

S: Look...

L: I am.

S: Don't interrupt. As I was about to say, blind people live perfectly well, but nobody lives without eating.

L: Doesn't mean that they taste.

S: That's where I come in.

L: People see, but they don't perceive.

S: People eat, but they don't taste.

L: You know, doctors are pushing low-sodium diets these days, but nobody can have too much light.

S: You want to bet? *(Indicates to audience that he's got a set-up.)*

L: *(self-righteously)* I don't gamble.

S: *(Pauses as he rolls eyes up, then continues thought.)* Why do people wear sunglasses?

L: *(smugly)* So you can't see their eyes.

S: No! So you can't dot their eyes. *(Shows glee in the play on words.)*

L: Okay, let's get serious.

S: Truce?

L: Truce.

S: Like Peter and Paul...

L: Without Mary?

S: I thought we were going to be serious.

L: Sorry. Go ahead.

S: As I was saying, Peter and Paul disagreed about how to spread the gospel and so decided to divide the work. Likewise, Paul and Barnabas disagreed on. . .

L: Paul had trouble getting along with people, didn't he?

S: *(looking seriously at Light)* That will be enough of that.

L: Forgive.

S: The world needs Salt and Light.

L: In the right amount.

S: In the right places.

L: For the glory of God.

S: Salt, which adds flavoring, leavening, preservative, is for the internal body. It represents what is needed in our lives and churches to grow strong and useful for God's purposes.

L: And Light represents our sharing the gospel with the rest of the world, showing the way to salvation.

S: Jesus used these elements which stimulate the senses of seeing and tasting to describe Christian imperatives.

L: Is that sound doctrine?

S: Will you cut it out! Say good night, Light.

L: Good night.

GATES AND ROCKS
by Matt Tullos

Dramatic parable

Adapted from: *Matthew 7*

Cast: *Narrator; Actors 1, 2, 3 (the character of Jesus), and 4.*

Narrator: Enter through the narrow gate, for wide is the gate and broad the way which leads to destruction.

Actor 1: Hey, it's open. Wow!! This is great!

Narrator: And many enter through it.

Actor 1: Come on, guys; there's plenty of room in this party! *(He walks through the imaginary gate and then mimes being destroyed.)* Hey! Wait a minute... this isn't what I expected. *Augh!!*

Actor 2: *(She mimes squeezing through an imaginary gate, straining as she speaks.)* But small is the gate and narrow the road which leads to life and very few find it.

Actor 3: *(This is the character of Jesus.)* Not everyone who says to Me—

Actor 4: *(in a whiney voice)* Lord, Lord—

Actor 3: Will enter the Kingdom of Heaven, but he who does the will of my Father who is in heaven. Many will say to Me in that day—

Actor 4: Lord, didn't You see me at church a bunch? I've been to church camp, disciple training seminars, Christian techno new wave psychedelic pretribulation rock concerts. I even know what the book of Obadiah is about. I was even planning to attend the Southern Baptist Convention; but then, of course, You came...

Actor 3: Leave!

Actor 4: Excuse me?!

Actor 3: Away from Me, you evil doers.

Actor 4: Don't You know who I am?

Actor 3: I never knew you.

Narrator: As Jesus continued to speak, the people were amazed.

Actor 3: Therefore—

Narrator: Jesus concluded,

Actor 3: Everyone who hears these words of Mine and puts them into practice is like a wise man who builds his house on the rock.

*Actor 2 becomes the house; the **other actors** personify the storm.*

Narrator: The rain came down, the streams rose...

Actor 2: Somebody get a bucket!

Narrator: And the winds blew and beat against the house. *(Actors beat on the back of Actor 2.)*

Actor 2: Help!! I don't think I can make it.

Narrator: Hold on to the rock!!

Actor 2: I'm trying!

Narrator: But it did not fall!

Actor 2: Whew! That was close!

Narrator: It did not fall because its foundation was on the rock.

Actor 3: But everyone who hears these words of Mine and does not put them into practice is like the foolish man—or woman, whichever the case may be—who built his...

Actor 2: or her...

Actor 3: house on sand.

Actor 2: Sand?

Actor 3: Sand. *(Actors mime action of storm with Actor 1 as house.)*

Narrator: The rain came down,

Actor 1: I love the rain.

Narrator: and the streams rose,

Actor 1: I think I can, I think I can.

Narrator: and the winds blew...

Actor 1: No, not the wind! Anything but the wind!

Narrator: and beat against the house...

Actor 1: Help me! Please!

Narrator: and it fell with a great CRASH!

Actor 1: Crash! *(falling to the floor)*

Actor 3: He who has ears to hear...shhh...listen.

HAPPY AND HOPPY
by Darlene Tullos

Fun drama about the power of affirmation

Cast: *Narrator; twin kangaroos Happy and Hoppy, Kangaroos 1, 2, and 3. Could use for Puppets.*

Setting: *They should begin down center stage facing the front. Kangaroos #1, #2, and #3 should begin upstage left behind a box large enough for all three to stand on the box at once, if possible. The Narrator should begin far left stage. These characters should be played with affirmation and energy!*

Narrator: Once upon a time, on the outskirts of the land of Australia, there lived twin kangaroos—Happy and Hoppy. Unfortunately, however, as fate determined, they were separated when they were only infants.

Happy and Hoppy are standing in the middle of the stage facing the audience.

Hoppy: Goodbye, Happy!

Happy: Goodbye, Hoppy!

Both make crying noises and hop to opposite sides of the stage. Hoppy turns back to audience. Happy faces the audience. Three other Kangaroos surround Happy, standing on chairs or boxes behind him.

Narrator: Happy found himself surrounded by balcony kangaroos. Now balcony kangaroos are those kangaroos who expect the best of their fellow kangaroos and encourage them to be the best they can be.

Kangaroo #1: Happy, you are such a wonderful kangaroo. I'm glad we're friends.

Kangaroo #2: You can do it, Happy. I bet if you try, you could hop higher than any other kangaroo. Come on, Happy, give it a try.

Kangaroo #3: That's right Happy. You've got what it takes. Hop, Happy, hop. Hop, Happy, hop.

All three Kangaroos join in chanting, "Hop, Happy, hop." Happy begins to hop. He hops several times, higher each time. He is smiling with joy. All actors freeze at the sound of the Narrator's voice.

Narrator: Happy was so fortunate to have such friends. With their encouragement, he learned to hop higher and higher, and eventually reached the extreme peak of his potential. Happy was happy.

Happy lifts his arms into the air proudly, then crosses them with glee and freezes. As narration begins, the three Kangaroos move to the other side of the stage and surround Hoppy , who then faces the audience. Happy turns back to audience.

Narrator: However, Happy's twin kangaroo, Hoppy, ended up on the other side of Australia and encountered quite a different environment. It seems that Hoppy was continually surrounded by basement kangaroos. Now basement kangaroos are those kangaroos who destroy the confidence and achievement of their fellow kangaroos, not intentionally, of course. They speak harshly from the basement and the effects are sad indeed.

Kangaroo #1: Oh, Hoppy, you'll never make it. You really should be hopping a lot higher at your age.

Kangaroo #2: That's right, Hoppy, I was told that you really don't give your all to hopping. You'll never amount to much at that rate. You might as well give up now.

Kangaroo #3: I've always had my doubts about you, Hoppy. Now I see that what I always thought is true. You probably won't be able to hop at all before long!

*All freeze when **Narrator** speaks.*

Narrator: Poor Hoppy! He began to believe those basement kangaroos, and although he had the potential to hop very high, he was destroyed by the doubt and insensitivity of his fellow kangaroos. He shriveled under their influence.

Hoppy: I'm me-e-e-e-e-e-elting!

Hoppy shrivels to the floor like the wicked witch in the "Wizard of Oz."

Narrator: So the encouraging words of the balcony kangaroos made Happy the best kangaroo he could be. But the harsh words of the basement kangaroos stifled Hoppy forevermore.

Kangaroo #1: *(stepping forward)* So, the moral of the story is:

Kangaroo #2 *(stepping forward)* Make "Happys," not "Hoppys" of those around you.

Kangaroo #3: *(stepping forward)* Live in the balcony of those you love, and avoid getting "caught" in the basement.

MILLY AND JAKE ON EASTER
by Zack Galloway

Cast: *Milly, Jake. Could be used with Puppets.*

Milly: Spring

Jake: Spring

Milly: What a wonderful time of the year. Flowers

Jake: Baseball

Milly: Fresh air!

Jake: Weed whackers

Milly: Weed whackers?

Jake: You know. Heavy fishing wire that rotates at over 5000 RPMS to destroy unwanted ugly weeds near the side walks and the flower beds.

Milly: Must be a "guy thing."

Jake: What?

Milly: Never mind. The climax of spring for me is the celebration of Easter.

Jake: I know all about Easter. See, first there was this bunny. I'm talkin' about this BIG bunny. He got really bored one morning so he got all the eggs from the chicken farm. He dyed all the eggs different colors and hid them all over the place.

Milly: Jake!

Jake: Then he got really hungry! So he turned all the bunnies in the neighborhood into chocolate.

Milly: What?

Jake: They sell 'em in stores you know. Then the kids found out about the egg business. So they started looking all over the place for eggs! And then—

Milly: *Hold it*!

Jake: What's the matter? I'm not finished with the story!

Milly: I'm not talking about some Bunny tale. I'm talking about the true story of Easter. Now, listen close Jake. The true story of Easter is the story of Jesus. Now listen in and try not to ask so many questions.

Jake: I'm all ears!

At this point have the teacher tell the story of the resurrection (possible form Matthew 28).

THE XMAS SIGN
by Ralph Dewey

Wanda catches on to Christmas

Cast: *Puppets Jerry, Torri, Wanda*

Scene: *A Christmas tree and a sign hanging over the **Puppet** screen that says, "Merry Xmas" on one side (and "Merry Christmas" on the other side for use later in the script).*

Jerry: Look at the Christmas Tree. Isn't it beautiful?

Torri: It sure is. I like the Christmas season the best. *(noticing the "Merry Xmas" sign)* Look at this sign. It just burns me up when they spell it X-M-A-S!

Jerry: I know what you mean. Do you know what burns me up?

Torri: No. What?

Jerry: A little chimney fire. It melts all the candy in the stockings.

Torri: I'm serious, Jerry. I don't like it when people leave Christ out of Christmas.

Jerry: Well actually, I don't like it either. I'm afraid that Christmas is becoming more and more like an excuse to go shopping instead of a celebration of Christ.

Wanda enters.

Wanda: Ask me what I like about Christmas?

Torri: OK. I'll play your little game. What do you like about Christmas?

Wanda: I like the gifts, the snow, the mistletoe, the toys, the lights, Rudolf the Red Nosed Reindeer, all the great food, Christmas presents— did I mention *gifts*?

Jerry and Torri: *Yes*!!

Wanda: I'm a little sad this year because my uncle hasn't rotten his usual Christmas letter.

Torri: You mean written don't you?

Wanda: No, I mean rotten. He hasn't sent a letter with money in it this year and I think it's *rotten!*

Jerry: Are money and gifts all you can think about?

Torri: Yeah! Don't you realize why we celebrate Christmas? It's the birth of the Savior of the world! Jesus Christ!

Wanda: Sure, sure, sure, but listen to this poem that I just wrote:
> Christmas is the best time of the year.
> It's when neat gifts suddenly appear.
> Each night I dream of a mountain of toys!
> None of which I will share with the boys!
> And there's only one thing I've got to say.
> Why can't it be Christmas every day?

Jerry: See what I mean? All you think about is getting gifts. Don't your remember what Jesus said? "It is more blessed to give than to receive."

Wanda: That's right. He did say that.

Torri: Since you like games so much, I've got one for you.

Wanda: Great. Next to getting gifts, I like games best.

Torri: Look at this sign and tell me what's missing.

Wanda: *(reading it.)* Merry Xmas. I know. I know. They left out the period at the end. Right?

Torri: That's not it. The answer is that they left Christ out of Christmas.

Jerry: This the way it should read. *(He flips over the sign which now reads "Merry Christmas.")*

Torri: That's much better.God gave His Son, Jesus to the world. It's Jesus' birthday. How would you like it if you had a birthday and no one invited you to the party?

Wanda: I see what you mean. I guess Jesus would feel left out. Maybe I've been acting too selfish. I've got it! I'm going to celebrate Jesus' birthday by doing things the way he would want me to do them.

Torri: Now you've got the Christmas spirit. But remember, you've got to act like Christ all year long.

Wanda: So we can celebrate Christmas all year long!

Jerry: That's right!

Wanda: Hey why don't we go over to my house and gather some things together for the needy people in the community.

They exit while improvisationally talking of other ways to celebrate Christmas!

ANGEL GRAMS
by Rick Shoemaker

A light dramatic presentation of angelic missions

Cast: *Dispatcher Angel, Gabriel, Angels #1, # 2, #3, #4. Could be used with **Puppets**.*

*Open with several **Angels** seated in a row, apparently waiting for an opportunity to do some important work. The phone rings and the **Dispatcher** answers.*

Scene I

Dispatcher: Angel Grams, Head Dispatcher Eli speaking. Oh, yes right away Sir. *(pause)* Not right away? *(pause)* Oh, I see. You prefer a series of messages. Now if you'll just give me the messages, the dates, the places, and the addresses, I'll see they are taken care of right away. Oh, you'll call me. That will be fine. *(pause—writes)* A message to Isaiah in Samaria, 742 B.C. *(pause)* Yes, yes, yes, this is great news. I'll send one of my best messengers with this one, Sir. I'll look forward to hearing from you again. *(hangs up phone)* Angel Number Three, a very special assignment for you.

*Eagerly **Angel #3** takes the Angel Gram.*

Angel #3: Yes, sir!

Dispatcher: Now, this is a very important assignment, direct from the top. Read it back to me to be sure you've got it right.

Angel #3: Yes, sir! "Therefore, the Lord himself shall give you a sign. Behold a virgin shall conceive and bear a son, and shall call his name Immanuel." *(Isaiah 8:14, KJV)*

Dispatcher: Go now, Isaiah waits.

Angel #3: Yes sir! *(leaves)*

Lights out.

Scene II

Phone rings.

Dispatcher: Angel Grams. Yes, Sir! Your last message was well received. I sent one of my very best angels. The next message already! I have several capable workers available. Ready sir *(writes)* Yes, yes, got it. Thank you for your confidence. *(looks over angels—calls out)* Angel Number Two please.

Angel #2: Yes, sir. Ready and willing to be of service.

Dispatcher: We got another Priority One! This is addressed to the Prophet Micah, 710 B.C. *(Hands the message to **Angel #2**)*

Angel #2: No problem Sir. I'll rush it to him right away.

Dispatcher: Read it to me first. We can't allow any mistakes.

Angel #2: "Thou Bethlehem Ephrathah, though thou be little among the thousands of Judah, yet out of thee shall he come forth unto me that is to be ruler in Israel." *(Micah 5:2, KJV)*

Dispatcher: Very good.

Angel #2: Does this mean He has chosen to make His arrival in little Bethlehem? Why such a small, insignificant place? Why not in a great city like Babylon?

Dispatcher: If He chooses Bethlehem, who am I to question? Just take this message to Micah.

Angel #2: I didn't mean to question, but I am surprised. I'll do as you ask. *(leaves)*

Lights out.

Scene III

Phone rings.

Dispatcher: Angel Grams. Head Dispatcher speaking. Good to hear your voice again. Gabriel? Yes, sir, he's available. I know. He is one of the best. Personally? Why of course. *(calls out)* Angel Gabriel, front and center.

Enter Gabriel.

Dispatcher: Headquarters for you.

Gabriel: Yes, sir. *(pause)* I'd be honored. Let me write this down—I've got it. To Daniel, in Babylon, 555 B.C. Yes, I'll do my best.

Dispatcher: Well, what is it? *(all Angels gather around, envious)*

Gabriel: It's His E.T.A.

Angel #4: What's E.T.A.?

Gabriel: You know, Estimated Time of Arrival. This will let the prophet Daniel know when He will make his appearance down there.

Angel #4: So when is that?

Gabriel: Well, it says *(reads)* "From the time the walls of Jerusalem are rebuilt until the Messiah comes will be 62 weeks of years." *(Daniel 9:25, KJV)* So He will come about 43 years after the walls are rebuilt in Jerusalem.

Angel #4: But that isn't scheduled around 440 B.C. or thereabouts?

Gabriel: Yes, so I've heard. Then He will be there at the beginning of the first century. I must hurry to Daniel with this news!

Angel #4: *(to himself)* Three priority Angel Grams and I got none!

Lights out.

Scene IV

Phone rings.

Dispatcher: Angel Grams. Head Dispatcher speaking. I thought I'd be hearing from you soon, Sir. Gabriel. He's right here. *(calls out to Gabriel)* Call for you Gabriel.

Gabriel: *(over phone)* I was hoping you would call on me again. Thank you for your trust in me. Where was that? Nazareth in Galilee. Mary of the house of David. I've got it. I'm on my way!

Dispatcher: What is the message?

Gabriel: He's going there very soon. I am to tell a young virgin that she shall conceive and bear a Son, called Jesus. I must hurry!

Angel #4: Why Gabriel again?

Dispatcher: Jealousy Number Four? It caused Old Lucifer to fall!

Angel #4: Not jealousy, I just want to be useful.

Dispatcher: Your time will come.

Lights out.

Scene V

Phone rings.

Dispatcher: Angel Grams. Thank you, Sir. Our personnel are highly trained. *(pause)* Yes, I see the problem. I've got just the angel for you. Specializes in dreams. Let me double check— that's Joseph of Nazareth. Got it. Talk with you later. *(calls out)* Angel Number Two front and center.

Angel #2: Yes, Sir.

Dispatcher: We've got a rather delicate problem. In Nazareth, Joseph is deeply troubled by the condition of his bride-to-be. He is thinking of breaking their betrothal and letting Mary go live somewhere so she won't have to handle the gossip. You must make Joseph understand what is happening. Can you handle the assignment?

Angel #2: Yes. I think so.

Dispatcher: This is Priority One, Number Two.

Angel #2: I understand. *(leaves)*

Angel #4: When can I go on Priority One?

Dispatcher: Patience, Number Four.

Angel #4: But it will all be over soon. He'll have arrived and I'll have done nothing to prepare His coming!

Dispatcher: Your time will come. Wait and see.

Lights out.

Scene VI

Dispatcher: It has happened! It has happened! The Messiah is born.

All the Angels gather, except #4 (who is out of the room).

Angel #2: May we all proclaim the birth?

Dispatcher: Yes, Number Three you go first. Tell the shepherds on the hills of Bethlehem. No one else is awake at this hour, and besides they will travel and tell others. After your lead, Number Three, the rest of you join in the glory of the celebration!

Dispatcher: Here is the birth announcement. *(Hands #3 a piece of paper.)*

Angel #3: *(reads)* "Fear not, for behold I bring you good tidings of great joy which shall be to all people. For unto you is born this day in the city of David, a Savior, which is Christ the Lord. And this shall be a sign unto you; You shall find the babe wrapped in swaddling clothes, lying in a manger." *(Luke 2:10-12, KJV)*

Dispatcher: "Now, go! Make haste!"

All leave, a short pause, then enters #4.

Angel #4: Where is everyone?

Dispatcher: To proclaim in chorus the wonderful news!

Angel #4: What news?

Dispatcher: The news of Immanuel! Christ is born!

Angel #4: Oh no! It's happened and I missed it all. I'm a failure as an angel! Nothing, but Priority Fours and Fives. Not a single Priority One.

Dispatcher: Number Four, it's true that nothing so big as this has ever happened before but who knows what may yet occur? Your time will come.

Lights out.

Scene VII
Sound of emergency buzzer.

Dispatcher: *(answers emergency phone)* Yes. Right away. I understand. I'm kind of short on help at the moment. All right. *(hangs up)* Number Four.

Angel #4: Yes, sir.

Dispatcher: This is Priority One Emergency.

Angel #4: Yes, Sir!

Dispatcher: Get to Joseph in Bethlehem immediately. King Herod is seeking to destroy the young child, Jesus. You must warn him to flee to Egypt before it is too late.

Angel #4: But a Priority One Emergency? What about Gabriel? He's better qualified.

Dispatcher: Gabriel is busy. It's up to you Angel Number Four.

Angel #4: All right. I'll do my best. Thank you, sir! *(leaves)*

Enter other **Angels.**

Dispatcher: Angel Number Four is on the way.

Gabriel: Yes, Number Four will do well.

Dispatcher: In fact, I'm already expecting a call saying all's clear.

Angel #2: How do you know?

Dispatcher: Just heard that King Herod's departure was put on the master calendar in headquarters. So Mary and Joseph and the baby should get the word before they unpack in Egypt.

Gabriel: It's good to know headquarters has everything under control.

Angel #3: "Glory to God in the highest and on earth peace good will toward men!" *(Luke 2:14, KJV)*

Ho! Ho! Ho!
by Christy Doyle

Cast: *Elf, Santa, Harry. Could use Puppets.*

Setting: *Santaland in a department store. Santa is seated in a throne and an Elf is next to him.*

Elf: I wonder where all the little kiddies are? I think I'm going to go out and have a smoke during this lull in the action.

Santa: You really shouldn't smoke.

Elf: Yeah, and you really shouldn't be so fat. Since when is it Santa's job to offer health advice?

Santa: *(Waves to a child we cannot see.)* Ho-ho-ho, Merry Christmas.

Elf: That's right, Santa, stick to the ho-ho-ho's. That's what you're good at.

Santa: I don't just make toys all year. I care about all the boys and girls.

Elf: Boy, you're really into this job, aren't you?

Santa: It's not a job, it's a way of life. I love children.

Elf: Please—gimme a break!

Santa: You can go on your break now if you'd like.

Elf: No, come to think of it, I'm gonna take my break when it's really busy. Is that okay with you, Fatso?

Santa: That doesn't insult me, you know. God made me this way.

Elf: Yeah, I guess that proves that God does make mistakes, huh?

Santa: Never.

Elf: Yeah, well I'd like to see your latest cholesterol reading.

Santa: Ho-ho-ho. Now who's giving advice?

Elf: Look, I'm tired of people telling me to stop smoking. If I want to die of lung cancer, it's my life.

Santa: But Ellie's praying for you.

Elf: Yeah, well Ellie is just a little six-year-old girl—hey, how do you know about Ellie?

Santa: Why, I'm Santa Claus. I know about all children.

Elf: Will you cut the Santa Claus garbage. I don't like the fact that you know anything about my little girl. How do I know that you're not some strange stalker? How long have you been on this job?

Santa: This is my first assignment.

Elf: What do you mean "assignment?" You talk like you're some secret agent guy or something.

Santa: Ho-ho-ho, Merry Christmas! *(He waves to another unseen child.)*

Elf: You make me nervous, Jelly Belly . . . Where are all the kids today? Usually this place has a line all the way to Sears.

Santa: You can't buy Ellie's gift at Sears. She wants you to stop smoking and go to church with her—not necessarily in that order.

Elf: Will you stop talking about Ellie? You are one strange dude.

Santa: Ellie asked for nothing for herself for Christmas—just you. She loves you.

Elf: And I love her.

Santa: Then give her what she wants for Christmas.

Elf: She'd be better off without me.

Santa: No, she needs you. Go to church with her. Get your life in order.

Elf: I want to—but I don't know how—listen to me, I'm pouring my heart out to Santa Claus! It's a good thing there aren't any children around.

Santa: No, but you are surrounded by love. Would you like some time alone?

Elf: Yeah, thanks. You go ahead and take your break. *(Santa exits.)* That is one strange guy. But, I guess he's right. Ellie does need me.

*A store clerk named **Harry** enters.*

Harry: Hey, Chris, what are you doing?

Elf: Okay, Harry, very funny. What does it look like I'm doing, playing golf? I'm waiting for some kids to see old Santa.

Harry: Santa called in sick today. Santaland is closed.

Elf: What do you mean Santa is sick? I was just talking to him.

Harry: No way, man. Santa called in sick. You better stay away from the bottle. The next thing you know, you'll be seeing angels! *(He laughs.)* Yeah, Santa and his sleigh of angels! *(He exits laughing.)*

Elf: Angels? *(He looks heavenward and freezes.)*

JUST WEST OF BETHLEHEM
by Matt Tullos

Shepherds from the West!

Cast: *Josiah, Henry, Jake, Angel Gabriel*

Josiah: And before I knew it, that wolf done snuck up behind me and started carryin' the sheep off by the scruff of the neck, one by one.

Henry: That ain't right and you know it! You were out like a light! How would you know? You were snorin' so loud that I couldn't sleep and it was your watch that night.

Josiah: I wasn't snorin'. I was clearin' my sinuses.

Henry: For 15 minutes!?

Jake: You got some sinus problem, boy.

Josiah: Well, you sure didn't seem like you were in too much of a hurry to help.

Henry: I woke you up, didn't I?

Josiah: How many times do I have to tell you? I wasn't sleepin'!

Henry: Well, tell Jake about what you did after that.

Jake: Hold it.

Pause. Light angelic music is heard and its volume slowly increases.

Henry: What was that?

Josiah: Sounds like—

Jake: Music! And—

Josiah: What's that light?

Henry: Angels! Great heavens!

Josiah: Great heavens is right!

Henry: Boy! Are we in trouble now!!!

Jake: Head for cover!

Josiah: Come back here, Jake! This ain't no thunderstorm!

Henry: *(trembling with fear)* Jehovah, forgive me for breakin' the Sabbath two weeks ago. Forgive me for eating that bacon when I went to Samaria! And for yelling at my wife last Thursday and for—

Jake: Will you cut it out? That angel is trying to say something to us.

Gabriel: Don't be afraid!

Josiah: You ain't gonna kill us?

Gabriel: I bring you the most joyful news ever announced and it is for everyone! The Savior—yes, the Messiah, the Lord—has been born tonight in Bethlehem.

Henry: The Messiah? Our Savior? Well—uh—*that's great!!*

Jake: How're we gonna know who He is?

Gabriel: Your will find the baby wrapped in a blanket and lying in a manger.

Heavenly music.

Josiah: Wow! Listen to all those angels!

Henry: Praise God! The Messiah is here!

Josiah: What's Messiah mean?

Henry: I'll tell you later. Would you look at all those angels!

Sudden silence.

Jake: Hey! Where'd they go?

Josiah: They plum vanished into thin air!

Henry: Well, what are we waiting for? Let's go see this baby!

Josiah: You never did tell me about who the Messiah is!

Jake: We'll tell you on the way.

Josiah: What about the sheep?

Henry: Forget the sheep! We just saw angels flyin' round in the sky and you're worried about sheep!

Jake: Besides, after all that bright light, they'll be stunned for days.

RECIPE FOR LOVE!
by Christi Enss

L ooking for the ingredients of a good marriage?

*A man dressed as a Chef stands in front of the congregation. Various cooking utensils are placed on a table in front of him. A big bowl takes up the bulk of the space on the table. It is surrounded by three measuring cups marked, **mutual trust, encouragement, love and respect**. As the chef talks about each item, he will pour the contents from the measuring cups into the big mixing bowl.*

Good morning! I'm the Wandering Cook, Pierre I Do, and I want to welcome you to "Basting, Sautéing, and Pickling Your Way to a Great Marriage." For today's selection I've chosen a recipe straight from the Master Chef himself. It's sure to spice up your marital life. It has all the ingredients for a loving relationship.

You know a good marriage doesn't just happen. It takes a combination of the freshest products. Just as soup and salad complement a main dish...so should a couple in love.

Let's get started, shall we? First let's begin with an essential ingredient. A little thing I call *mutual trust*. I have a friend right now whose marriage could use this very thing. His wife doesn't trust him at all. In fact, he calls his wife American Express because he can't ever leave home without her. Trust keeps a marriage from going bad. Proverbs 31:11 says, "The heart of her husband doth safely trust in her, so that he shall have no need of spoil." This is a key element to remember. I don't think they make a Tupperware dish big enough to keep a marriage from drying out.

Next, we add some *encouragement*. Try praising your spouse, even if it does frighten them at first.

I know a man who never gave his wife an ounce of encouragement. One day she'd had it. When he came home from work that day, he found his bags packed and waiting for him. His wife said, "Honey, I don't know how I'm ever going to get along without you, but starting tomorrow I'm going to try!"

After encouragement, generously pour a large helping of *love* and *respect* into your mixture. This will make all the difference to the endurance of your dish. After several years of marriage I can still say I love my wife, no matter how heated up things get at times. When I got married I closed the door to every woman in the world; and since then I haven't even peeked through the keyhole.

My wife and I have survived because I know that a good woman inspires a man. A brilliant woman interests a man. A beautiful woman fascinates a man. But it's the sympathetic woman who gets him.

Ephesians 5:33 tells us that, "Nevertheless let every one of you in particular so love his wife even as himself; and the wife see that she reverence her husband."

After you have all the necessary ingredients mixed together, your dish should be able to withstand being baked, chilled, souffléed, or smothered in onions.

I'm the Wandering Cook. Remember the goal in preparing a well seasoned marriage is not to cook alike, but to cook together.

Bon appétit!

Nooo Problem!
by Randall and Arinée Glass, and J. Scott Reynolds

Where do you place your faith?

Purpose: *To show where we as Christians get our help.*

Adapted from: *1 Peter, John 3:16, Proverbs 3:5-6*

Cast:
#1: Female who places all faith in astrology
#2: Male who places all faith in Christ
#3: Male who places all faith in fortune cookies

Staging: *#2 is center stage slightly downstage from #1 and #3 who are on either side of him.*

Props: *Fortune cookies, telephone, and Bible*

#2: *(holding Bible)* When my sister needs guidance and wants to know what to do, she calls her astrologer.

#1: *(dialing phone)* 1-900-DE-STARS. Shoot! Busy. *(redials)* 1-900-DE-STARS. What am I going to do? It's busy! *(getting frantic; redials)* 1-900-DE-STARS. Hello, hello? Hold? Okay. *(pause)* Hello, yes? I need to know my future. *(pause) Wow!* I'm going to have a good day today? Great. Also, who will I date next? Shoot. They put me on hold again. I can't believe this is only $4.99 per minute.

#2: But when I need guidance—no problem—I just go to my Heavenly Father in prayer and trust Him to guide me. Now my cousin, when he needs some encouragement he turns to . . .

#3: Fortune cookies. *(starts cracking several open and reading the piece of paper inside each)* No, no. I don't like this one. No, this one's not good either. Oh, here's one—"Your smile is your best asset." That's it! How encouraging!

#2: But when I need encouragement—nooo problem—I just turn to God's Word and that tells me that God loves me so much that He sent His only Son to bear my sins, so I can have the best life ever. The Word also says that God cares so much about me that He knows everything about me, even how many hairs are on my head!

So whenever you need encouragement, feel lonely, need guidance and care, just say—noooo problem!—and put your trust in God through prayer and His Word. NOOOO PROBLEM!

TIME OUT!
by Matt Tullos

Getting your church off of the bench

Cast: *Announcer, Coach, Smith*

Announcer: This one will come right down to the wire, sports fans! There are 30 seconds left on the clock and the game is tied. The Tigers are in trouble. They have only five players eligible and only four on the court. The Tigers' coach is calling time out.

Coach: What's wrong, Smith?!

Smith: Oh, nothing. Just watching the game.

Coach: Johnson fouled out!

Smith: Yeah. Too bad. What are you going to do?

Coach: What am *I* going to do?

Smith: Yeah.

Coach: What do you think I'm going to do? All our players except five have fouled out of the game! And you're one of those five! Get out there!

Smith: But Coach, when I joined the team, I really wasn't expecting to play.

Coach: What!?

Smith: I just wanted to be a part of the team! You know—sit on the bench—wave the towel—listen to you during timeouts rake the other guys over the coals.

Coach: I don't believe this! It's the most important game of the year!

Smith: I know!

Coach: Then get out there!

Smith: But, Coach, we might lose If I go out there. Basketball isn't my physical gift.

Coach: Physical Gift? What are you talking about?!

Smith: Now waving the towel, sitting on the bench, listening to you call plays—those are my physical gifts.

Coach: I don't care what your, as you say, physical gifts are. Get out there!

Smith: Now hold on one second! Who do you think you are?

Coach: I'm your coach. Remember?

Smith: Some coach you are! Telling me what I should do. I might just have to visit some other teams! I can't believe it. I come to most of the practices. I show up for all of the games! I keep track of the scores. I never get in anybody's way and you have the gall to blame me just because I don't want to play in the game! You're worse than my pastor!

FISHERS OF MEN
by James Tippins

A fun illustration of barriers to evangelism

Cast:
Fisherman
Trout
Bass
Crab
Salmon
Minnow
Speaker

Setting: *A man in fisherman's gear is fishing.*

Props: *Fishing pole, cardboard cross, sign with fish name on each*

Fisherman enters with pole, whistling. On the end of the hook is a cardboard cross. The **Fisherman** *throws the line over a railing, which represents the water. Whenever a fish comes up, a person nearby holds up a sign which shows what type of creature is being talked to.*

Fisherman: I hope the Lord blesses me with a catch today.

Trout: *(popping his head out of the water)* Hey, keep it quiet up there, I'm trying to get some sleep.

Fisherman: I'm sorry, but . . . . *(with a sudden thought)* would you like to be caught today?

Trout: No way! I'm too tired from last night's party to come with you today. *(He disappears back in the water.)*

Fisherman: *(unperturbed)* I hope the Lord blesses me with a catch today.

Bass: *(popping his head out of the water)* You know you'll never catch anything like that.

Fisherman: *(startled)* Why not?

Bass: Because I'm much too strong for that flimsy line; and besides, your bait tastes terrible.

Fisherman: I'm . . . *(The* **Bass** *disappears, cutting off the* **Fisherman**.*)*

The fisherman's line begins to pull/release/pull/release. The **Fisherman** *gets excited and* **Crab** *pops his head out of the water letting go of the line. The* **Fisherman** *stumbles.*

Crab: Hallo, you don't know how to do anything right do you?

Fisherman: *(confused)* What do you mean?

Crab: I mean fishing. If you can't do it right, then you shouldn't do it at all.

Fisherman: But the Lord told me how . . .

Crab: Hey, testings *my* job . . . and maybe you should find another! *(He disappears.)*

Fisherman: I hope the Lord blesses me with a catch today.

Salmon: *(pops his head out of the water, breathing heavily)* Hey, get that thing out of my way, I'm in a hurry.

Fisherman: Would you like to be caught today?

Salmon: No way José, I've got too many things to do, like getting upstream. See you later. *(He swims upstream.)*

Fisherman: I hope you do have a chance later.

*(As the **Fisherman** looks out over the congregation, the **Minnow** pops his head out of the water.)*

Minnow: *(clearing his throat)* Ugghhhmm . . .

Fisherman: *(looks at **Minnow**)* Hello?

Minnow: Hello.

Fisherman: Would you like to be caught today?

Minnow: Why?

Fisherman: Because God loved the world so much, that He gave His only Son, so that if you believe in Him, you will not die, but have life forever.

Minnow: That's what I've been looking for.

Fisherman: What?

Minnow: Well, let's go!

*The **Minnow** grabs the line and pulls it taut. The action freezes as the **Speaker** steps up to the platform.*

Speaker: "Blessed are the poor in spirit, for theirs is the kingdom of heaven." *(Matt. 5:3, NIV)* And He also said, "Come, follow me. . . and I will make you fishers of men." *(Matt. 4:19, NIV)*

DON'T DUCK THE DUCK
by Buddy Lamb

G ood Samaritan parable like you've never heard before!

*This is to be acted out as the narrator tells the story. Words in **italics** are to be read with emphasis. There can be much interplay between the narrator and the characters. It is a loose version of the "Good Samaritan" from Luke 10:30-38. Good for **Puppets**.*

Cast:
Narrator
Mr. Duck: *The Victim*
Two Sly Foxes: *The Robbers*
Ms. Deer: *The Priest*
Mr. Skunk: *The Levite*
Old Hound Dog: *The Good Samaritan*
Tom BoBear: *The Inn Keeper*

Narrator: One day, **Mr. Duck** was taking a trip south. I think he was going to *Dizzy World*. On the way, **Two Sly Foxes** came up to him and robbed him, beat him, and left him for a *dead Duck*.

A little later, **Ms. Deer** came by and saw the almost dead **Duck**. She could have helped him because she had lots of *bucks,* but she didn't, she just said:

Ms. Deer: Dear me.

Narrator: And then she walked on by.

After that **Mr. Skunk** came down the path and saw **Mr. almost dead Duck,** and he said:

Mr. Skunk: My, my what have we here?

Narrator: He turned up his nose as he walked away and said:

Mr. Skunk: This really *stinks!*

Narrator: After the *dear Deer* and *stinkin' Skunk* had *ducked* the *almost dead Duck,* an old *Hound Dog* came along. He knew the *Duck* was almost dead and The *Hound Dog* said:

Hound Dog: What can I do *I ain't nothing but a hound dog.*

Narrator: But he could not just *duck the Duck* so he got his *band—ages* and helped him up.

The old *Hound Dog* did not take him to the *Heart Break Hotel,* he took him to **Tom BoBear**'s hotel where he had *left the light on.* It was called *Holiday Den.*

The Hound Dog: Tom, if he needs more help, call a doctor, and don't put it on the duck's *bill,* I'll pay for it.

Tom BoBear: Don't worry, I'll call the *quack.*

Narrator: The old *Hound Dog* did not *duck the duck,* but he was the duck's friend.

The moral of this story is:

> When you see someone down on their Luck
> And you just want to say "Oh Yuck,"
> To be their neighbor, you can't pass the Buck,
> Just remember, *Don't Duck the Duck!*

JAMES: THE MOVIE!
by Matt Tullos

A bonus one act on the book of James

Cast: *Film reviewers* **Gene** *and* **Roger**; *Floor Manager; Four actors who play multiple roles,* **Alan, Bill, Clark, Dana** *(female)*

Props: *two swivel chairs, clapboard, pointing stick*

Setting: *Gene and Roger are in swivel chairs on stage right. They speak directly to the audience.*

Gene: Good evening and welcome to our weekly movie review show: *"In the Bible."*

Roger: Tonight we'll be taking a look at the spicy, energetic, and sometimes shocking book of James.

Gene: Shocking is right, Roger. Theologians through the centuries have marveled at the implications of the tiny epistle.

Roger: Of course, Gene, you can't forget the practical message of James. He had much to say to his readers.

Gene: Maybe a little too much.

Roger: What do you mean by that?

Gene: Don't you think James was a little hard on those early believers?

Roger: Hard? You're out of your mind! James is no harder than any of the other early biblical teachers.

Gene: We could argue about this all night—let's roll the clip from the first chapter.

Roger: O.K., Gene. In this scene, the book opens as James discusses the joy of trials and difficulty of doing.

Gene: If you look beyond some of the truly wacky illustrations and a few cinematic flaws, the message rings loud and clear.

Roger: Let's watch.

Floor Manager: (with a clapboard—very loud) James, Chapter 1, Verse 2, Take 1—Roll-um!

Lights up on actors.

Alan: Consider it pure joy when you face trials of many kinds.

Three people line up as if to race. These people are sluggish and reluctant. **Bill, Clark,** *and* **Dana.**

Bill: Oh, brother, not another race!

Clark: Come on, Coach!

Dana: My legs, my aching legs!

Alan enters into the line, bouncy and enthusiastic.

Alan: Another trial, praise the Lord! *(to audience)* For you to know that the testing of your faith develops perseverance.

Bill: I don't think I have a chance.

Dana: My right ankle is weak. I'm sure it's going to twist, if I give this race my all.

Clark: Why didn't I take up chess?

Alan: With God's help, I will be victorious. I can do all things through Christ. He is my strength!

Bill: Who is this guy?

Alan: *(to audience)* For most of us, trials are not simply athletic events. Trials are found mostly in the main event—life itself.

Each speaks to God

Bill: Another baby! We're going to have another baby!?!

Clark: This is the third time my brakes have gone out! *(in desperation)* God, where are you?

Dana: God, I wanted to be the head cheerleader—now I'll never get a date. My life is over!

Alan: God, thank you for allowing me to face difficulty. I'm learning so much. Thank you for making me adequate for all situations I'll face.

Break to next scene.

Bill: If any of you lacks wisdom, let him ask of God who gives to all without finding fault, and it will be given to him.

Alan goes to Dana

Alan: If I were you, I would sell now. The house is kind of new, and interest rates are really low. It would be an easy sell.

Clark goes to Dana

Clark: Don't sell; wait 'til the market settles down. You'd be a fool to sell now.

Alan to Clark

Alan: You're crazy. If she sells now, the chances are she'll be able to move into a bigger house for much less.

Clark: That's the most absurd thing I've ever heard—don't sell!

Alan: Sell!

Clark: Don't sell!

Sandwiching Dana

Alan: Sell!

Clark: Don't sell!!

Bill: Wait!!! If anyone lacks wisdom, let him ask of God.

Alan, Clark, and Dana: God??!

Bill: But when he asks, let him believe and not doubt, because he who doubts is like a wave of the sea, blown and tossed by the wind. Let no such man think he shall receive anything from the Lord. For he is hesitating, unreliable, and uncertain about everything he does.

Dana: I guess I'll sell. No, I'd better wait. Maybe I should leave. No, I'd better not. Can I just stay here while I think about it—?

Clark: No, you can't. *(showing watch to Dana)* Look at what time it is, and we're only on verse 8.

Break to next scene.

Alan: *(to audience)* Let the person in humble circumstances glory in his elevation. Wesley Grey—where are you?

Bill: Here I am.

Alan: Well done, Wesley. You cleaned the floor of your church every week. And when someone was in trouble, you were always the first one to volunteer your time and effort. Your spirit of helpfulness and forgiveness endured throughout your entire life. Receive your reward.

Bill (Wesley) is handed an imaginary crown that seems very large.

Bill: Lord, there must be some mistake. I don't deserve this crown.—I was the church janitor. I was never elected a deacon. I figured I'd be sweeping up around here too.

Alan: Wesley, receive the fruits of your labor.

Bill (Wesley) receives his reward as he falls to his knees.

Alan: (to audience) And the rich in being humbled should glory, because, like a flower, he will pass away. (to players) Anthony Klein—Where are you?

Clark: (as Anthony)Oh, no need in going over all those great achievements of mine. I realize that my work as chairman of the committee on committees was indispensable, and, of course, my wealth added a certain, uh . . . prestige to the church, and . . . well . . . the reward shall be sufficient enough.

Clark (Anthony) holds out his hands as if to receive a huge crown. Alan hands him an imaginary key ring.

Alan: Those are the keys to Wesley Grey's kingdom car. Drive him to his mansion, will you?

Break from the scene.

Dana: The sun comes up and parches the grass.

Bill: Its flower falls off,

Clark: and its beauty fades.

Alan: Even so, will the rich man die in the midst of his pursuits?

Dana: Blessed is the man who is patient under trial and stands up under temptation. Let no one say, when he is tempted,

Bill: "The Lord tempted me!"

Dana: He, Himself, tempts no one.

Break to next scene.

Bill: (walks to a chair and sits down) Honey, I'm home. (picks up imaginary book—to himself) Oh, great. Maybe I'll have time to catch up on my Bible readings. New Year's resolutions never come easy.

Alan walks in limping, hunched, and evil-looking. He is a demon, preparing to snatch a victory from the Christian. His voice also is evil-sounding. He sneaks up behind Bill.

Alan: TV—TV—TV—

Bill: (pause) I think I'll watch some TV.

Bill walks up to Clark who is squatting down in the form of a TV. Bill turns Clark "on" and Clark plays a preacher on TV.

Alan: No!!! (He hides his face from the TV screen and then chants.) MTV! MTV! MTV!

Bill: I don't think I want to hear Billy Graham again. I think I'll watch some . . . (a thinking pause) MTV.

Alan (Demon) grimaces and rubs his hands with delight. Bill changes channels, and Clark is transformed into a closeup of a rock start. Scene closes to a freeze at the sound of Dana's voice.

Dana: Every person is tempted when he is drawn away, baited, and enticed by his own evil desire!

Break freeze.

Alan: For every good and perfect gift is from above, coming down from the father of lights with whom there is no variation or shifting shadow.

Dana: Every good and perfect gift?

Clark: (in a moment of discovery) Hey, that's right! For God so loved the world that he gave!

Alan: Exactly!

Bill: Hold on.

Dana: And the fruit of the spirit is love, joy, peace—

Bill: Hold it! (angrily) Now this is a play about James. How are we going to get through the first chapter if you keep jumping from John, to Galatians, to who knows what next?!?! (others are stunned) Now where are we?

All three surround him.

Alan: Let everyone be quick to hear—

Clark: Slow to speak—

Alan, Clark and Dana: Slow to anger!

Bill: (sheepishly) *Sorry!!*

Break to next scene.

Dana: Okay., Guys. It's time to start class. Many of you might be wondering, "Why should I do push-ups?" Well, we at the American push-up school believe that there is no better way to tone . . .

Others: (enthusiastically) Tone!!

Dana: Strengthen!

Others: Strengthen!!

Dana: And develop good bicep and pectoral muscles. Now last week we saw those wonderful videos, "Push-ups—It's Not Just an Ice Cream Bar," and "Jane Fonda's Push-up-a-cise." The week before that we looked at several push-up charts, and we even read from the Push-up Handbook. And today, we shall begin doing push-ups. Well, actually, you will do some. I have an important meeting to attend. We are having a push-up teachers convention in Atlanta, and my plane leaves in 15 minutes. I'm sure you can survive without me. (She exits from the scene.)

Bill: I think I've bruised my thumb from writing all these push-up notes. I'd better wait to do push-ups. See you guys later! (He exits from the scene.)

Alan: I missed the videos last week. I think it would be wise for me—

Clark: I know.

Alan: Well, I'll see you next week!

Clark: (He speaks as he does push-ups.) Prove yourselves doers of the word and not hearers only. (jumps up) But one who obeys the work, not having become a forgetful hearer, but a diligent doer—(flexes a bicep) he shall be blessed!

Lights off actors.

Floor Manger: O.K.! That's a take!

Roger: As far as the direction and force of the message, I definitely give it a thumb's up.

Gene: It's controversial and risky. I can see where some pastors would shy away from James.

Roger: But, Gene, over 50% of all Baptists are non-resident members. The modern church is in need of a message on "doing."

Gene: You're right, Roger. Thumbs up for me, too.

Roger: We now have a special treat here at "In the Bible." A rare visit with the director of this production . . . A cinematic celebrity in his own right, (Name of the Drama Director).

Gene: Thanks for stopping by.

Director: Sure.

Roger: Let's get right to the point. What is the directorial responsibility to the homiletical and yet hyper-practical motivation of a canonized treatise written by the brother of piosity incarnate?

Director: (confused) Say what?

Gene: I think what Roger means is that this is a tough assignment for a tough director. Do you have—well, let's say—the right stuff?

Director: Well, yes— I—

Roger: Thanks, Mr. (Director's Name).

Director: But . . .

Gene: Let's take a peek into chapter 2.

Roger: In this chapter, James deals with faith and partiality.

Lights on actors.

Dana: My brothers, don't hold your faith in Christ with an attitude of personal favoritism.

At this point, Clark acts the part of the rich man; Alan, the poor man; and Bill, the pastor.

Clark: For if a man comes into your assembly with a gold ring and dressed in fine clothes . . .

Alan: (in country accent) And there also comes in a poor man in dirty clothes,

Dana: And you (pointing to Bill) pay special attention to the rich one saying:

Bill: You sit right here next to our associate pastor. Have you met our financial chairman? He's leading our "Together We Spend" program.

Dana: And you say to the poor man, who possibly doesn't look or smell like your average deacon—

Bill: Oh yes, we have a special and important duty for you. We want you to be chairman of the terrorism committee. There have been several terrorists threats within the U.S., even some in Texas. What we want you to do is stay outside near the parking lot and look out for anyone who looks suspicious.

Dana: If you really keep the royal law found in the Scripture, "Love your neighbor as yourself," you are doing right, but if you show favoritism—you sin.

Clark: (getting down on all fours) For whoever keeps the whole law and yet stumbles at one point. . .

Bill walks across the stage, not looking down, not watching where he is going. He then stumbles over Clark.

Bill: Whoa! (stumbling)

Dana, Clark and Alan: . . . is guilty of stumbling over the whole law.

Dana, Clark, and Alan fall to the ground. All Actors freeze.

Lights up on Gene and Roger.

Gene: Wait! Freeze that shot—right there.

Roger: What's the problem, Gene?

Gene: Let's rewind that scene a little.

All the Actors reverse their action to the place where the dialogue begins just as if they were on video.

Clark: For whoever keeps the whole law and stumbles at one point—

Bill: Whoa!!

Dana, Clark, and Alan: . . . is guilty of stumbling over the whole law. (Actors freeze.)

Gene: Well, What about that!

Roger: What about it, Gene?

Gene: That's quite a revolutionary statement.

Roger: Oh yes, the underlying meaning is definitely one of grace.

Gene: That's what I wanted to emphasize. We can't be self-righteous. We can't say we're better than others, because all of us have sinned. And sin—

Roger: Is sin. But by God's grace we are victors. This scene also shows the athletic ability of the actors. Let's watch that last bit of action in slow motion. And notice the symbolism in action—each actor representing a law as it crashes to the ground.

Actors fall down in slow motion.

Gene: A great scene!

Roger: A great moment!

Gene and Roger: Thumbs up!!

Lights down on Gene and Roger.
Break to next scene.

*In this next scene, **Alan** narrates the action as the Actors mime the illustrations. **Alan** takes on the character of an old schoolmaster with a pointing stick.*

Alan: When we put bits into the mouths of horses to make them obey us, we can turn the whole animal.

Dana: *(on Bill's back)* Hi Ho—Silver, away!!

Alan: Or take ships as an example. They are so large and are driven by strong winds, yet they are steered by a very small rudder wherever the captain wants to go.

*Actors with body movement create a ship using one of their feet as a rudder. **Clark** is the captain.*

Clark: Thar she blows!

Alan: Likewise the tongue (**Actors** *stick out their tongues as **Alan** points to them with pointer*) is a small part but boasts great things.

Break to next scene.

Dana: We only had four people come to church visitation. The pastor was really sad. *(This is said to Alan.)*

Alan: *(to Bill)* We only had a few people at church visitation. The pastor was grieving.

Bill: *(to Clark)* The pastor is leaving!

Clark: *(yelling it to everyone)* Hey—the pastor is leaving!

Dana: You're kidding!! Where did you hear that?

Clark: Oh, from a very good source, I assure you. It's strange, I saw him the other day. He seemed happy. His secretary had just finished the church bulletin. She's been sick all week. The pastor said he missed her hard work.

Dana: *(to Alan)* The pastor's secretary is back. The pastor said He missed her.

Bill: The pastor kissed her. *(to himself—then to Alan)* The pastor kissed the secretary?

Alan: Where did you hear that?

Bill: From a very reliable source, I assure you.

Actors freeze.

Dana: The tongue is a small part of the body.

All: But it makes great boasts.

Clark: The tongue is a fire.

Bill: It has the potential to create a world of evil.

Dana: It corrupts the whole person.

Alan: It sets the whole course of his life on fire. But the wisdom that comes from above is first

Dana: Pure,

Alan: then

Clark: peaceloving,

Bill: considerate,

Dana: submissive,

Clark: full of mercy,

Alan: and

All: good fruit.

Actors freeze.

Lights up on Roger and Gene.

Floor Manager: That's a take!! *(He brings out a water cooler and a sponge. Actors sit down, rest, and recuperate.)*

Roger: Chapters 2 and 3 of James. How about it, Gene, do you feel the modern interpretation is accurate to the biblical context?

Gene: Well, Roger, I'm a little confused and disappointed.

Roger: Why?

Gene: Well, the editing is a little shoddy, don't you think? I mean, the cinematographer even filmed the water breaks!

The Actors look at the Critics and then jump back into place and freeze, away from the acting area.)

Roger: Yeah, that's more like it! Overall the message of the tongue hits a little close to home.

Gene: Sure does, Roger. The message seems to be—cut out the slander, backbiting, and vain words.

Roger: Submit to God.

Gene: And be full of his wisdom.

Roger: *(jokingly)* Maybe we should become movie actors. *(They both laugh.)*

Gene: But our jobs would be in danger at the *Sunday School Sun* and the *Christian Tribune*.

Roger: And the Christian Movie Critic Market is really tight right now.

Gene: So, back to the show—the last segment. Chapters 4 and 5 deal with the boasting of believers and the servanthood of suffering. Here are a few scenes from James 4 and 5.

Floor Manager: James 4 and 5. Take 1. Roll 'um.

Break to next scene.

Alan: What causes quarrels among you?

Dana: *(as a child)* I want your doll!

Clark: *(as a teen)* I want a car like his!

Bill: *(as an adult)* I want your job!

Alan: Don't they come from desires within you?

Dana, Clark, and Bill: Yes.

Alan: You do not have because you do not ask of God.

Each speaks to God.

Dana: I want her doll.

Clark: Can I have a car just like his?

Bill: Lord, let me be an executive in this company.

Bill, Dana, and Clark freeze.

Alan: When you ask God, you do not receive because you ask with wrong motives that you can spend what you get on your own pleasures.

Bill, Dana, and Clark break their freeze.

Bill: Submit yourselves to God.

Dana: Resist the devil,

Clark: and he will flee.

All: Submit to God.

Dana: Now listen to those hypocrites who say,

Clark: *(in a preachy voice)* Next year the ministry of our church will explode. We shall send missionaries to Indonesia and build the largest racquetball arena in the south.

Dana: *(to Clark)* You don't even know what will happen tomorrow. What is your life?

Clark: Why, how dare you question my life. I am one of the premier evangelists of the city, maybe even the state!

Bill: You are a mist that appears a little while and then vanishes.

All: Submit yourselves to God.

Alan: Instead, you should say, "If it is the Lord's will, I shall do this or that . . ."

Break to next scene.

Bill: Now listen, rich people, weep and wail because of the misery that is coming upon you.

Dana: Over 900 million people live on less than 75 dollars a year.

Bill: Now listen, rich people, who have hoarded your wealth in the last days.

Clark: Now listen, rich people, who turned away from—Bangladesh, Somalia, Haiti, and Bosnia. You sing a song to feed them and leave.

Bill: You have lived in luxury and self-indulgence.

Alan: Poverty brings illiteracy, disease, and brain damage.

Bill: Now listen, you have condemned and murdered innocent people who were not opposing you.

All: Now listen!!

Pause, then break.

Alan: Be patient, brothers, until the Lord comes.

Dana: He is like a farmer who waits for land to yield its valuable crop.

Bill: You, too, be patient; stand firm because the Lord's coming is near.

Clark: Don't grumble against others or you will be judged.

All: The judge is standing at the door.

Alan: *(pointing to the side)* Hey, would somebody get that door?

Actors freeze.

Floor Manager: That's a take!

Gene: Well, that's the book of James.

Roger: I wonder if we could ask the actors some questions.

Gene: Roger! That's a *film*!!

Roger: I know. But they were so convincing! Let me give it a try. Hey!! Can you hear me?

The Actors look at each other.

Clark: Yes sir?

Roger: Could we ask you a few questions?

Dana: That's highly unusual.

Clark: Give him a break.

Alan: Yeah, go ahead.

Roger: These are just a few practical questions that you didn't cover. First of all, what should I do if I'm in trouble?

The Actors confer.

Clark: Pray.

Roger: What should I do if I'm happy?

Bill: In that case you should . . . sing a song . . yeah, that's it . . . and uh, praise the Lord.

Roger: Well, I'm not that much of a singer, but I'll give it a try. Do you have any questions, Gene?

Gene: Sure. Who could pass up an opportunity to actually talk to a film! My question is, what should we do if we are sick?

Actors confer with each other again.

Dana: We believe you should call on the people of your church. Let them anoint you with oil. Your faith will heal you.

Bill: We might also remind you about what we said earlier about not presuming on God's sovereignty.

Clark: Right.

Alan: Remember how Elijah prayed? He prayed that it wouldn't rain, and it didn't. Then he prayed that it would rain, and it did! A five-star performance, if you ask me.

Clark: But that's another film altogether.

Roger: Well, thanks guys. And that's our show this week. Definitely a thumb's up book for me.

Gene: Me too, Roger.

Roger: So that's it, folks, until the next time we'll see you *"In the Bible."*

Easy Indexes
For Subject
and Scripture!

Subject Index

M ore specific themes and where to find them.

Puppet Scripts Index

These 26 scripts can easily be adapted for Puppets.

Scripture Index

Handy references to help plan worship experiences.